ANSWERS IN TIME
A Layman's Apologetic

Ryan Domenick

BALBOA.
PRESS

A DIVISION OF HAY HOUSE

Balboa Press books may be ordered through booksellers or by contacting:

Balboa Press
A Division of Hay House
1663 Liberty Drive
Bloomington, IN 47403
www.balboapress.com
1 (877) 407-4847

Because of the dynamic nature of the Internet, any web addresses or
links contained in this book may have changed since publication and
may no longer be valid. The views expressed in this work are solely those
of the author and do not necessarily reflect the views of the publisher,
and the publisher hereby disclaims any responsibility for them.

The author of this book does not dispense medical advice or prescribe the use
of any technique as a form of treatment for physical, emotional, or medical
problems without the advice of a physician, either directly or indirectly. The
intent of the author is only to offer information of a general nature to help
you in your quest for emotional and spiritual well-being. In the event you use
any of the information in this book for yourself, which is your constitutional
right, the author and the publisher assume no responsibility for your actions.

Any people depicted in stock imagery provided by Thinkstock are models,
and such images are being used for illustrative purposes only.
Certain stock imagery © Thinkstock.

Printed in the United States of America.

ISBN: 978-1-4525-2323-1 (sc)
ISBN: 978-1-4525-2324-8 (e)

Library of Congress Control Number: 2014917998

Balboa Press rev. date: 10/15/2014

The urge to find a way out of this impasse ought not to be dampened by the fear of incurring the wise rationalist's mockery.

- Erwin Schrodinger

Contents

CHAPTER 1

THE WRONG QUESTION

David Hume, possibly the greatest skeptic to ever write stuff, still has the best summary of the problem. "Is he willing to prevent evil, but not able? Then he is impotent. Is he able, but not willing? Then he is malevolent. Is he both able and willing? Then whence evil?"

For those who don't speak in eighteenth century dialect, a more common version of the problem is often stated like this: "How can I believe in a god who ..."

Fill in the blank. There's a lot of terrible stuff that happens. Really terrible. From the grand scale of human history like the Holocaust and the Crusades, to terrible tragedies happening right now, to individuals, in the first world. In places like America.

There are people in this world that have it far worse than I do. People living in the third world, facing the constant threat of starvation or genocide or enslavement. People surrounded by disease and poverty. I can't pretend to be able to empathize with them.

That being said, I know pain. Physical, mental, and spiritual pain, all rolled up in a ball of hatred and depression. Hopelessness and despair. I know what it's like to want desperately to believe in a good and loving God, when everything around you is telling you he isn't there. And if he is there, he is, at best, indifferent. I know what it's like to scream with desperation into the void, and receive nothingness as an answer. I get it, is what I'm saying. I have asked the question, "How can I believe in a God who…"

For many years, I fought the question away. I stifled my own intellect. I didn't search for the answer, because I was afraid of it. I heard a lot of standard empty quotes like "Trials bring you closer to God" and "Prayer isn't for God. It's for you." I hated those answers.

Then one day, I decided to find the real answers. I decided to stop fighting the question. I decided I didn't care what answers I found. I didn't care where the journey ended. If God wasn't real, I wanted to know. I stopped looking for comfort and started looking for truth. Admittedly, being raised in a Christian home, I was probably biased from the start, but I still think I found the right answers.

The first and most important thing I realized was that I was asking the wrong question. "How can I believe in a God who …" is really two different, and very good questions rolled up into one dumb one. If it is indeed God who is doing whatever it is the asker is referring to, then necessarily he must exist. So the two questions at stake here are:

1. Is there a god?
2. Is God evil? (This of course becomes irrelevant if the answer to the first question turns out to be "no.")

More specifically for question number two, is a good God compatible with the existence of evil? It is difficult to separate the question out like this in the middle of crushing pain and anger. I understand. You want an answer, you want it simple, and you want it now. So did I. But if I really wanted answers, I had to ask the right questions. I didn't know that I had started a journey that would last the better part of a decade, and really, is still ongoing. I didn't know the mountain of philosophy, cosmology, and metaphysics that stood in front of me that I would have to knock down to an understandable level.

In the coming pages, I'll describe that journey. And it will probably become obvious to you, humble reader, that I am woefully unqualified to write this book.

CHAPTER 2

SURVIVING THE FIRING SQUAD

I remember hearing several times when I was a kid about the remarkable precision of the earth's orbit around the sun. People said that if it were a few thousand miles closer to the sun, we would all burn. If it were a few thousand miles farther away, we'd all freeze to death. The remarkable precision was supposed to point to design. To a designer. To God.

Then, of course, I found out that scientists have known since the seventeenth century that all of the planetary orbits are elliptical. Every year, our distance from the sun varies by about three million miles, and that distance doesn't even effect the seasons. Isaac Newton described the orbits mathematically to near perfection with his law of universal gravitation (the only modification being a correction for Mercury's orbit explained by Einstein's general theory of relativity.)

But, as wrong as that was, the universe is incredibly fine tuned in all kinds of even more intricate and amazing ways. By the way, I'll be dealing exclusively with cosmology in this section. I'm not going to touch on biology. Evolution, while important to understand and discuss, will take me down a long and convoluted rabbit hole that would take too long and add little to the discussion, mainly because the definition of evolution is so vague. When scientists talk on evolution, it is often difficult to tell if they are talking about simple genetic variation, descent with modification, natural selection, the thesis of common ancestry, Darwinism, Neo-Darwinism, or even the naturalistic origins of life. Indeed sometimes you can detect scientists moving between many of these distinct hypotheses in a single talk. The point is, for my purposes here, it doesn't matter.

The Numbers

So, let's talk about some numbers. Numbers that had to be unimaginably specific for you to be sitting here reading this. I've already mentioned Newton's law of universal gravitation, so we might as well start with gravity. The law says that any two objects will attract each other with a force that is directly proportional to the product of their masses and inversely proportional to the square of the distance between them. So it's mass number one multiplied by mass number two divided by the square of the distance between the masses. Then you take that result and you multiply it by the gravitational constant (G). And G just so happens to equal about $6.67 \times 10^{-11} Nm^2kg^{-2}$. N is newtons, which is how you measure force. M is meters, and kg is kilograms. So G=0.0000000000667.

G is really small, and it has to be. Gravity is one of the four fundamental forces, the others being electromagnetism, the strong force and the weak force. The strong force keeps the nucleus of atoms bound together, and the electromagnetic force keeps the whole atom and molecules together. (The weak force governs the decay of subatomic particles and isn't very relevant for this discussion.)These forces are a lot stronger than gravity. A whole lot stronger. 10^{36} times stronger. That's why you didn't have to factor in gravity when you were learning about chemical bonds in high school.

The only thing gravity has going for it is that it doesn't have a north and a south pole like a magnet. Gravity always attracts. So while electromagnetism can cancel itself out, gravity always gets stronger as mass gets bigger. So eventually, when things get big enough, gravity takes over as the stronger force. But they have to get really big.

Here's why it's important. Let's imagine a world where G isn't quite so small. Say it's only 10^{30} times weaker than electromagnetism. Now objects don't need to get as big for gravity to win. Stars and planets would be a billion times smaller. Nothing bigger than insects could ever evolve on those planets. Gravity would crush anything bigger. Even insects are unlikely, because the lifetime of stars would only be around 10,000 years, which is not near enough time for any sort of evolution on planetary bodies. Galaxies would form really fast, they would be small, and stars would constantly collide with each other. If G is big, we don't exist.

Here's an example that's even more incredible. G is only bounded on one side. We couldn't exist if it were any bigger, but we could still find ourselves here today if it were smaller. But $\mathcal{E}$ is bounded on both sides.

$\mathcal{E}$ is the nuclear efficiency of helium, which isn't as hard to explain as it sounds. The sun and all stars are nuclear fusion machines. The immense heat and pressure fuse hydrogen atoms into helium atoms. A hydrogen atom is made of one proton and one electron (most of the time.) A helium atom is made of two protons, two neutrons, and two electrons. Einstein's most famous equation, $E=mc^2$, tells us that mass has a lot of energy stored in it. To get an idea of just how much energy is contained in matter, rocket fuel releases barely a billionth of its rest mass energy. The only way matter could be completely converted to energy would be an encounter with anti-matter. Anti-matter has 100% efficiency. Nuclear fusion of hydrogen to helium has a 0.7% efficiency. So $\varepsilon = .007$. Compared to anti-matter, it's not great, but compared to rocket fuel, it's a nice improvement to say the least.

What this means is every helium atom weighs 99.3% as much as the protons and neutrons that made it. The rest of the mass is converted to heat, which is why the sun is kind of hot. This is this number that determines the lifetime of a star.

The creation of helium depends on the strength of the strong force, which is what binds the nucleus of atoms together and determines the amount of energy required to break them apart. Or in other words, the strong force determines the value of ε. A helium atom is assembled in stages. Hydrogen first gets an extra neutron. Scientists call that deuterium, or heavy hydrogen. (Scientists aren't always creative.) Now let's imagine a world where $\varepsilon = .006$ instead of .007. The strong force is no longer strong enough to hold the neutron to the proton, and the path to helium is cut off before it ever gets started. The entire universe would be hydrogen. Life wouldn't exist. Chemistry wouldn't even exist.

What about if $\varepsilon = .008$? The way the universe is now, two protons repel each other (because of the electromagnetic force) so strongly that the strong force can't bind them together without the aid of at least one neutron. But if $\varepsilon = .008$, the strong force gets the edge over electromagnetism, and protons start sticking together. In the early universe, this would have happened really quickly. There would be no hydrogen left today. Thus there would be no water. There would be no fuel for stars. There would be no life. ε has to be exactly what it is: .007.

Here's an example that's even more incredible. It involves an extremely delicate balance between three different constants.

Ω (omega) is the symbol assigned to the critical density of the universe. The universe is expanding, as determined by the red shift in light from distant stars and galaxies due to the Doppler Effect, which states that a wave frequency will change relative to the motion of the observer. It's the reason sirens change pitch as the police pass by you and you sigh in relief as you realize they were chasing someone else. In the light spectrum, shortening the light wave causes it to turn more blue, and lengthening the wave causes it to turn more red. Everywhere we look in the sky, light is turning redder. The universe is expanding. The critical density is the amount of matter that would be required for gravity to halt the expansion, and it has been calculated. It's five atoms per cubic meter. Scientists have also calculated approximately how many atoms are actually in the universe, and found that if we disassembled all of the stars and planets and spread the atoms out individually and uniformly across the entirety of space, there would be about one every ten cubic meters. That's 0.2 atoms per cubic meter, which the reader will notice, is less than five. So if $\Omega=1$ represents the critical density of the universe, then the actual value of Ω is .04. A lot of scientists believe that there is enough dark matter to bring the value up as high as 0.3, but definitely not to 1. We are below the critical density. The universe will continue to expand forever.

The second constant in the balancing act is Λ (lambda), the cosmological constant. It was first thought up by Einstein, who didn't know that the universe was expanding. The prevailing thought at the time was that the universe was static, neither expanding nor contracting. Einstein realized that if that were the case, gravity would cause everything to contract, and we'd all eventually be crushed into a tiny ball. Since that wasn't happening, he postulated that there was a repulsive force that counterbalanced gravity, which he named the cosmological constant. He later called the idea the worst mistake he ever made. But recently, science has started to realize that Λ probably exists after all. It's really weak, and can only compete with gravity on super massive scales, but it's there.

The final constant (Q), is the ratio of how strongly gravity holds structures together (how much energy is needed break them apart) to their total rest mass energy. Q will change based on the size of the object, but for the largest objects in the universe, like clusters of galaxies, it's about 10^{-5}. Because Q is so small, the universe can safely be regarded as smooth, despite having stars and planets organized into galaxies and clusters. It's the same way the earth can safely be regarded as a sphere, even though up close the Rocky Mountains seem pretty big. But if Q were too small, no stars or galaxies would form at all. Due to the nature of gravity, tiny microscopic irregularities in the expansion rate in the early universe magnify into the enormous stars and galaxies we now observe.

The formation of galaxies requires that Ω, Λ, and Q not only be almost exactly what they are, but also that their ratios to each other be almost exactly what they are. Ω is about 0.3, but this means that it was much closer to exactly 1.0 in the early universe. As the universe expands, the gap between the energy of gravity and the energy of the expansion widens, so the fact that Ω is as close to 1.0 as it is, is very remarkable. It means that the expansion rate fell within a very tiny range. About one part in 10^{60}. If Ω had been just a little bit smaller, the universe would have expanded too fast, and no stars or galaxies would have formed. If Ω were a little bit larger, the universe would have re-collapsed before any life ever evolved. At the same time, Λ can't be too large or it would overwhelm G before any galaxies had formed. It had to be fine-tuned to about one part in 10^{120}. Still further, if Q were any smaller, if galaxies formed at all they would be very weakly held together and processed particles would not recycle into new stars. If Q were less than 10^{-6}, galaxies would never have formed in the first place. If Q were much larger, the initial irregularities would have quickly developed into black holes. If a galaxy managed to form, stars would be packed too close together to sustain any solar systems.

There are more examples, but they get progressively harder to understand without a physics degree, which I don't have. By now, you probably get the idea anyway. A lot of things had to go really well for us to be here. The important thing to keep in mind is that there is nothing in physics that requires the constants to be what they are. Nothing in the law of universal gravitation, for example, requires that $G=6.67 \times 10^{-11}$. So the next question that naturally comes to mind is, "How did everything go so right?"

The Options

There have been three different explanations offered to explain the precision of all of these universal constants: chance, necessity, or design.

Chance

A common objection at this point is that if every universe is equally probable, then an observer shouldn't be surprised to find himself in a universe that he can observe. The fancy name for this concept is the Anthropic Principle. It basically says that once we account for the fact that certain properties cannot be observed by us, since we can only observe properties that are compatible with our existence, we shouldn't be surprised to be living in a universe fine-tuned for us to be able to observe it. Therefore, no explanation is required. But there is a misguided equivocation here. An observer who evolved in a universe he can observe should indeed not be surprised that he finds constants there that permit his existence, but that doesn't mean it's probable that those constants exist.

One of the most helpful analogies I've read is The Firing Squad analogy. Suppose I'm a prisoner on death row, and today is the day I'm to be executed. I'm dragged in front of a firing squad of one hundred trained marksmen standing only a few feet in front of me, all of their rifles aimed perfectly at my chest. I hear the command, "Ready!" I will myself to accept my fate. I hear "Aim!" I close my eyes and brace for the end. I hear "Fire!" The deafening explosion of gunfire from one hundred rifles echoes through the air. I slowly open my eyes, and after a brief moment of denial and confusion, observe that I am still very much alive.

Should I then reason that I shouldn't be surprised? After all, if all of the marksmen hadn't all missed, then I wouldn't still be conscious to be surprised. Since I am indeed alive, is there then nothing to be explained? Of course there is! I shouldn't be surprised that I don't observe that I am dead, because that's impossible. But I definitely should be surprised that I do observe myself to be alive. The improbability of all one hundred marksmen missing is way too large to shrug off.

Many scientists recognize how unlikely the chance hypothesis is and have attempted to even the odds a bit with the Many Worlds Hypothesis. Using inflationary cosmology, which I'll give a brief explanation of later, they postulate that our universe is one of many existing in what is called a "false vacuum." (For a pretty understandable explanation of most of the ideas of inflationary cosmology, I'd suggest "Many Worlds in One" by Alexander Vilenkin, who championed the hypothesis.) In order to give enough time for enough universes to form, Vilenkin assumes a B-theory of time, so that universes that will form in the future to observers in our universe have already formed in that universe. Essentially, B-theory assumes that temporal becoming is illusory. Time is simply the fourth dimension of space, and the future already exists along that line. This is how time is regarded in relativity theory, and it works well in its equations. But whether it should actually be regarded that way is another discussion. It's a discussion that, in fact, I will be dealing with later in this book, because it is central to solving the second question. For now though, I'll set it to the side.

Even if we grant that the B-theory of time is correct, there is a larger problem with this version of inflationary cosmology, which Vilenkin calls "eternal inflation." If our universe is just one decaying spot in a sea of false vacuum that inflates forever, then it is highly improbable that we would observe the type of universe that we do. The region of space should be much smaller than it is. In fact, it is way more likely that the universe is the size of your brain, and everything around you isn't real. This concept is referred to as Boltzmann Brains, and I'll delve deeper into them later. It is also very likely that we would be observing really strange events, like a horse popping into being and then immediately disappearing from random collisions, because it's a lot more probable that that would happen than it is that all of nature's constants would fall into the life-permitting range. Since no one has ever observed anything like this ever, I think it's pretty safe to assume that eternal inflation doesn't explain fine tuning.

Necessity

Many physicists are searching for a Grand Unified Theory, or GUT. In the late 1800s, it was discovered that electricity and magnetism were both part of the same force that determined how positive and negative charges interact. The hypothesis of GUT is that electromagnetism and the strong and weak force may all be part of the same force, or at least they were all part of the same force in the early universe. Basically, there may be one basic force that governs the micro-world of sub-atomic particles. Still more speculative scientists search for a Theory of Everything, or TOE. TOE would incorporate gravity into the single fundamental force as well. The most promising candidate for a TOE is super-string theory, which would require that the universe have eleven dimensions. None of the extra dimensions have been found, nor has anyone come up with a way to find them. For a good explanation of why that's so hard to do, you can read Edwin Abbot's "Flatland," in which he describes a two-dimensional world where the inhabitants have no concept of a third dimension. Even if super-string theory is completely correct, is doesn't predict the universe we live in. In fact, string theory allows for about 10^{500} different possible universes, and the life-permitting number in that range is still really small, and might even be zero. All of this being considered, necessity seems pretty unlikely to me.

Design

That leaves us with what is, in my mind, the most intuitive explanation anyway. The intricate and delicate universe that we inhabit was designed so that we can live in it. A common objection at this point is that inferring a designer only pushes the problem back a step, because then we must explain who designed the designer. But in the rules of logic, in order to recognize an explanation as the best, you don't have to have an explanation of the explanation. In fact, if you always had to explain an explanation, it would lead to an infinite regress, and you could never explain anything. As an example, if you found a treasure in a cave, you would naturally assume someone hid it there, even if you had no idea who did.

Prominent evolutionary biologist Richard Dawkins objects that the designer would be just as complex as the universe, so no explanatory advance is made. This objection is flawed in a couple of ways. Simplicity is only one of the factors in weighing competing explanations, and it's generally considered less important than other factors like explanatory power and scope. But putting that aside, as the philosopher Dr. William Craig points out, the designer would be an unembodied mind, which is actually a very simple entity. It's not even a physical entity. It could and probably would have very complex ideas and thoughts, but the mind itself is about as simple as it gets.

The Watchmaker

What I've just described, though it factors in a lot of new science, is not a new argument. It's commonly referred to as the Teleological Argument for the existence of God. It was made famous by William Paley in the early 1800s. In his book, *Natural Theology*, he put it like this:

> In crossing a heath, suppose I pitched my foot against a stone, and were asked how the stone came to be there; I might possibly answer, that, for anything I knew to the contrary, it had lain there forever: nor would it perhaps be very easy to show the absurdity of this answer. But suppose I had found a watch upon the ground, and it should be inquired how the watch happened to be in that place; I should hardly think of the answer I had before given, that for anything I knew, the watch might have always been there. (...) There must have existed, at some time, and at some place or other, an artificer or artificers, who formed [the watch] for the purpose which we find it actually to answer; who comprehended its

construction, and designed its use. (...) Every indication of
contrivance, every manifestation of design, which existed in
the watch, exists in the works of nature; with the difference,
on the side of nature, of being greater or more, and that in a
degree which exceeds all computation.[1]

I think this two hundred year old argument is still a pretty
convincing one. If it were the only one, I would say that I'm pretty
sure that a god exists. But I know a god exists. Next, I'll tell you
why.

---

[1]   William Paley, Natural Theology, 1802.

Chapter 3

Hilbert and Tristram: BFFs

.

Modus ponens: the most basic form of a logically deductive argument is organized in three stages:

1. If a, then b.
2. a.
3. Therefore, b.

In deductive arguments, the conclusion follows necessarily from the premises. As long as premises can be shown to be more plausible than their negations (like "not a" in part 2), the conclusion is unavoidable. Now, there are lots of different kinds of logical fallacies one could commit when developing a modus ponens, the most common being what is called "affirming the consequent." This happens if you change the argument to

1. If a, then b.
2. b.
3. Therefore, a.

But as long as you don't commit any fallacies, a modus ponens is airtight. You can't dispute the conclusion if you agree that the premises are valid. The reason I know that a god exists isn't because "he lives within my heart." It isn't because I've "experienced" God, whatever that means. (I was never quite sure what people meant by that. You experience events. How do you experience a person?) God has never spoken to me. I know God exists because of the cosmological argument, which is a modus ponens. It goes like this:

1. Everything that begins to exist has a cause.
2. The universe began to exist.
3. Therefore, the universe has a cause.

If you want to make it follow the modus ponens format perfectly, you can re-phrase premise one as, "If something begins to exist, it has a cause." Both of these premises need and deserve a ton of discussion, and we are going to do just that. So here we go.

Premise 1

Premise 1, that everything that begins to exist has a cause, will take much less of our time, because if we deny it's truth, then it seems to me to be the same thing as believing in magic. If things can just pop into being uncaused, then there is no reason why this shouldn't happen all the time. If you can't accept premise 1, then you can't be surprised if an elephant appears on your lap right now. How did it get there? If you deny premise 1, you can't ask that question. Maybe there is no cause.

Premise 1 is called the casual principle. One objection to premise 1 that warrants a response is that the casual principle applies to everything in the universe, but not to the universe itself. In the same way that every part of an elephant may be light in weight, but that doesn't mean an elephant is light in weight. This is a common logical fallacy known as the "fallacy of composition." But the casual principle can't be dismissed when an object gets large enough. For example, suppose you found a small dark spherical object lying in the woods. You would naturally wonder what it was and how it got there. Now suppose the sphere was the size of your house. Does it become any less mysterious? Now suppose it's the size of the universe. It still needs to be explained. Premise 1 is a metaphysical statement. It necessarily applies to all of reality. Something can't come from nothing.

One even more common but very poor objection to premise 1 is the question, "Then who caused God?" This doesn't work for several reasons. Number one, this question is jumping ahead in the argument. Premise 1 has nothing to do with God. At this point in the argument, God isn't even a part of the discussion. But let's humor this objector for a moment. I would simply ask the objector to re-read the premise. It doesn't say, "Everything has a cause." It says "Everything that begins to exist has a cause." So if God began to exist at some point in time, then he would indeed need a cause for his existence. But God is traditionally understood as an eternal being. (What exactly I mean by "eternal" will be discussed a lot more.) He never started existing. He just exists. This objection miserably fails.

Another common objection in the scientific community is that quantum physics disproves premise 1, since events in the sub-atomic world are entirely random and unpredictable in a lot of ways. This objection also fails. "Random" and "unpredictable" are very different than "uncaused." Quantum fluctuations are indeed unpredictable, but they don't come to be out of nothing. Sub-atomic particles arise from fluctuations in the quantum vacuum.

And as we now know, vacuum contains energy. The reader will note that "energy" is certainly not "nothing."

Premise 1 of the argument is about as solid as any statement can be. Being doesn't come from non-being.

Premise 2: The Philosophy of Infinity

Premise 2 is where we will spend most of our time, because both philosophers and scientists have a lot to say about it. I'll look at what the philosophers have to say first. The philosophy of infinity is fascinating. (Well at least it is to me.) Basically, if infinity can't actually exist, then the universe can't be infinite, and therefore, must have a beginning. So let's see if that's true.

Potential and Actual Infinity

At first, you might think that an infinite number of things can definitely exist. There is obviously an infinite amount of numbers, for example. But there are two versions of the word "infinity," and they mean two very different things. One of them is symbolized by the standard symbol for infinity we all know: ∞. The other is represented by the Hebrew letter aleph, which looks like this: $\aleph$. ∞ is the symbol for a potential infinite. It's a set that constantly grows, but never reaches the infinite. Zeno's paradox of motion is based on a potential infinite. If Zeno had realized this, he would have realized that motion is actually very possible. Just because a line segment could be divided forever, doesn't mean you will ever arrive at an infinite number of divisions. A better term for ∞ is "indefinite." $\aleph$ is the symbol for an actual infinite. It stands for an infinite set of things. Premise 2 asserts that $\aleph$ is impossible in reality.

Some mathematicians assert that premise 2 has been proven false by the establishment of Georg Cantor's infinite set theory, but this objection assumes the objective reality of mathematical objects. This is a view that is controversial at best and outright false in some cases. $\sqrt{-1}$, for example, is impossible in reality but very useful in mathematics. Anti-realist views of mathematics hold that there are no mathematical objects. I think this is the preferable view, in large part due to the thought experiments presented below.

Philosophers have come up with a lot of thought experiments about what it would be like if an actual infinite really existed. My favorite one is "Hilbert's Hotel," thought up by David Hilbert. It goes like this.

Imagine a hotel that has an infinite number of rooms. Now suppose all the rooms are full. There are an infinite number of guests that night. Now suppose a guy walks up to the front desk and wants a room. "Sorry, we're all full," says the concierge. But then an idea strikes him. He decides to shift every occupant one room down the hall. Guy in room 1 moves to room 2, guy in room 2 moves to room 3, guy in room 3 moves to room 4, and so on, all the way to infinity. Now room 1 is open, and the new customer has a place to stay. But before he showed up, all the rooms were occupied, and no one left.

Now suppose an infinite number of new guests show up at the front desk wanting a room. The concierge then comes up with another brilliant idea. He shifts the guy in room 1 to room 2, then shifts the guy in room 2 to room 4, the guy in room 3 to room 6, and so on, all the way to infinity. Suddenly, every odd numbered room is open, and an infinite number of new guests get a place to stay for the night, even though the hotel was completely occupied and no one checked out. The concierge could repeat this process an infinite number of times, and always accommodate an infinite number of new guests.

Hilbert's Hotel gets even weirder when people start checking out. Suppose every guest in every odd numbered room checks out of the hotel. In other words, and infinite number of people have checked out. Logic dictates that the hotel should be empty at this point, but it obviously isn't. All the even numbered rooms are still occupied. The hotel is half full. But suppose the owner doesn't want a half full hotel. So he shifts the occupants in the reverse order from what he did before, and now suddenly every room is full again, even though no new guests checked in.

But now suppose that everyone in rooms 10 and up checked out at the same time. Now the hotel is almost completely empty, and there's nothing the owner can do about it. But the same number of people checked out as when all the guests in the odd numbered rooms left. In both cases, we subtracted the same number, but we got different answers.

What Hilbert is saying is that his hotel can't exist. It's logically absurd. It follows that the actual infinite is logically absurd. It can certainly exist in mathematics under a strict set of operational rules, but nowhere in reality. But if the universe doesn't have a beginning, then it has gone through an infinite series of events, which it can't do. Therefore, the universe has a beginning. The universe began to exist.

Shandy's Diary

But just for fun, let's pretend that an actual infinite can exist. The universe still had to have had a beginning, based on the impossibility of forming an actual infinite by adding members of a series one at a time. Regardless of how much time is available, you can never create an infinite set. If someone were counting to infinity, obviously, they would never reach infinity. But if the universe has existed forever, it has endured an infinite series of events. Before the present could occur, the event immediately prior had to occur, then the event before that, and so on to infinity. So one could never actually arrive at the present. But we are obviously in the present.

Here's a good example to drive this point home. Jupiter orbits the sun once for every 12 Earth orbits. (It's a little less than 12, but I'm rounding up for the sake of simplicity.) Let's imagine Earth and Jupiter have been orbiting the sun from past infinity. Which planet has completed more orbits? The natural answer would be Earth. It has completed 12 times as many orbits as Jupiter. But if both planets have been orbiting from eternity, then they have both completed an infinite amount of orbits. They have both revolved around the sun the exact same amount of times.

Here's another common example. In the 1700s, Laurence Sterne published "The Life and Opinions of Tristram Shandy" in nine volumes. In it, Tristram is unable to explain anything simply. He doesn't even get to the point of his own birth until volume three.

Now let's suppose Tristram Shandy is immortal, and he has been writing his diary forever. Let's also suppose it takes him about a year to describe one day of his life. When would he finish? According to the principle of correspondence, he should be finished today, because the number of days that have passed is the same as the number of years. They are both infinite. But this seems obviously false. Tristram couldn't have written today's events down. Every day of writing takes a year, so he would actually be infinitely behind on his diary. It's logically absurd.

But it's even more absurd than that. If the series of events in the past is infinite, then why didn't he finish his diary yesterday, or last week, or last year? After all, an infinite series of events had already passed yesterday. He should have already finished. In fact, he should have finished infinitely long ago. At any point in the past we go, we'll never find Tristram writing his diary. He's already finished. But how can he be finished if he was writing from eternity and it takes him a year to write down each day?

Forming an infinite from successive addition is logically absurd. It can't be done. But for the universe to be past eternal, it has to have happened. Therefore, the universe had a beginning. The universe began to exist.

CHAPTER 4

INFLATION AND COLD SHOWERS

*The heavens declare the glory of God. The skies proclaim
the work of his hands. Day after day they pour forth speech.
Night after night they reveal knowledge.*[2]

Not only do we know that the universe began to exist, but over
the past century, we've pretty much figured out exactly how it
happened, thanks to Einstein mostly. His General Theory of
Relativity (GTR) predicted something groundbreaking. The
universe was not stationary. It was not constant. It was not eternal.
GTR permits it to expand or contract, but not remain steady. In
the 1920s, a mathematician named Alexander Friedman and an
astronomer named Georges Lemaitre came up with solutions to
GTRs equations, and they both predicted an expanding universe.
Then, at the close of the 1920s, Edwin Hubble observed the
red shift. The light waves were stretching in all directions. The
universe was receding away from us. Einstein was right. Then, the
implications of expansion started to manifest.

---

[2]   Psalm 19:1-2

Premise 2: The Science of the Beginning

Genesis: The Bang

No one could ever observe the Big Bang from the outside. The most important part of understanding the theory is the right perspective. It's not an explosion of matter into space. It's the explosion of space and time itself. There is no outside. There is no before. What's more, when scientists say that the galaxies are receding, they don't mean the galaxies are doing so out into a previously empty space. It's space itself that is expanding.

So let's say we rewind the universe. It will contract. And it will keep contracting until we arrive at a state of zero space and an infinitely dense point of matter. Scientists call this point the singularity. A point, by definition has no dimensions. It takes up no space. There is no space around this point. The singularity is the beginning in every sense of the word. It is the edge of space and time. There was nothing before it.

"Hang on a second, Mr. Author," the astute reader says at this point. "Didn't we just finish proving that nothing can actually be infinite?" Yes we did, but it's ok to say the point is infinitely dense in this case, because a point has no dimensions. A point doesn't really exist. The singularity is the beginning of everything that exists, but it doesn't exist itself.

Cosmology, for a large portion of the twentieth and twenty-first centuries, has included a concentrated effort to come up with a working theory that avoids the beginning, because, I suspect, almost everyone understands, at some level, what this pesky point would imply.

The Alternatives

1. *Bouncing Bangs*

Remember that GTR allows the universe to contract as well as expand. So some scientists theorized in the 1960s that maybe it does both. Maybe eventually the expansion would halt and revert to a contraction. And maybe, if matter were not evenly distributed throughout the universe, then all the matter wouldn't meet at a point. Matter could pass by other matter and keep going into another expansion. And maybe the expanding and contracting went on forever.

This theory, called the oscillating model, was more or less abandoned when Roger Penrose and Stephen Hawking formulated their Singularity Theorems in the 1970s. While I wouldn't even pretend to try to understand the math, what they showed is that a singularity is inevitable no matter how the matter in the universe is organized. Even if there have been expansions and contractions, eventually, if we trace far enough back into the past, we will find a singularity. And if that weren't enough to convince everyone, scientists discovered in the 1990s that the expansion of the universe was accelerating instead of slowing down. So any hope of it ever contracting died. And so did the oscillating model.

2. *Imaginary Time*

We live in four dimensions. Space has three. Time has one. The time dimension is unique, in that it is directional. It always moves forward, unlike space, where you are free to move as you like. This is fortunate, because it means we can back out of our garages and stuff like that.

The reader will recall from Chapter 2 that inflationary cosmology does not regard time as directional. While inflationary theory is far from proven and has lots of competing versions, it is a good way to explain why the universe is as homogeneous (smooth) as it is, and it is pretty widely accepted, so for my purposes here, I'll assume it's true.

An interesting thing happens to the inflationary cosmology model if you substitute the time variable with imaginary numbers. It becomes indistinguishable from space. Another way to say this is that space takes on four dimensions and time disappears. Steven Hawking proposed that prior to the Planck time (10^{-43} second after the Big Bang) this is exactly what the universe was like; four-dimensional space. By solving the equations with imaginary numbers, the edge of spacetime is rounded off. It never comes to a point. The singularity disappears. This is supposed to show how the universe never had a beginning.

So let's assume for a minute that this model is accurate. It doesn't avert the beginning. Just because the universe didn't have a beginning point wouldn't mean it didn't have a beginning. So what if the beginning is rounded off? So what if we can't identify the exact point where it started? That hardly makes it infinite.

But maybe the problem is solved because the fourth dimension ceases to be time at all. As Hawking puts it in *A Brief History of Time*, "It would be neither created nor destroyed. It would just BE."[3]

But what exactly is imaginary time? It is certainly a useful mathematical device. But what is an imaginary second? Or an imaginary day? The champion of inflationary cosmology, Alexander Vilenkin, recognizes this in "Many Worlds in One" where he says, "This is not the kind of time you measure with your watch. It is expressed using imaginary numbers, like the square root of -1, and *is introduced only for computational convenience.*"[4]

---

[3]   Hawking, *A Brief History of Time*, 136
[4]   Vilenkin, *Many Worlds in One*, 182 (emphasis added)

What's more, when Hawking offers a non-verificationist explanation of this in his article *The Edge of Spacetime*, he contradicts himself. He writes:

> *"In the very early universe, when space was very compressed, the smearing effect of the uncertainty principle can change this basic distinction between space and time. It is possible for the square of the time separation to become positive under some circumstances. When this is the case, space and time lose their remaining distinction – we might say that time becomes fully spacialized – and it is then more accurate to talk, not of spacetime, but of four dimensional space. Calculations suggest that this state of affairs cannot be avoided when one considers the geometry of the universe during the first minute fraction of a second. The question then arises as to the geometry of the four dimensional space which has to somehow smoothly join onto the more familiar spacetime once the quantum smearing effects subside."*[5]

"*Once* the quantum smearing effects subside." According to his own theory, they never subside. There is no time. It is impossible for them to come to an end. At what *time* does four-dimensional space become spacetime? Spacetime cannot stand in any relation to Hawking's four-dimensional space because four-dimensional space has no time value. There are more versions of the inflationary cosmology scenario floating around, but this one is by far the most popular, and they all operate on the same basic premise. So I think it's safe to say inflationary cosmology leaves the beginning of the universe firmly intact.

---

5   S. W. Hawking, 'The Edge of Spacetime', in William Lane Craig and Quentin Smith, *Theism, Atheism and Big Bang Cosmology*, 317

Sticking with Einstein

So it looks like, for once, we got it right the first time. The universe is expanding. It's been expanding since the beginning, which was a singularity of infinite density and pressure. Einstein knew what he was talking about. As a final blow to any other possibilities, Vilenkin (the inflation guy), along with two other physicists, Alan Guth, and Arvin Borde, recently wrote up a theorem. They postulated stationary observers moving away from each other in an expanding universe, and one guy traveling past them at a constant velocity. Since the spectators are moving away from each other, if one of them measures the traveler's velocity as he passes, it will be smaller than the measurement of the spectator that measured it previously. The key insight is that as you approach infinity, due to the ever increasing speed of the traveler relative to any particular spectator, the traveler's clock will stay finite, due to relativity theory. (This is special relativity theory (STR), as opposed to GTR. I'll explain STR very soon. I promise.)

What this means is that as the expansion approaches infinity, the traveler does not. A contradiction is reached. Once again, when trying to create an actual infinite from successive addition, we encounter logical absurdities. Therefore, any universe that has been, at least on average, expanding throughout its history, cannot be infinite. So the theory applies even to the oscillating model, because the oscillations grow with each succession, and so they would average out to an expansion.[6] The theorem doesn't even require any of Einstein's equations to be true. In fact the math doesn't get any harder than high school level. The universe began to exist. Even if it began with a rounded end instead of a point.

---

[6]   Alexander Vilenkin, *Many Worlds in One*, 175-176

Even if there have been multiple big bangs. At some point in the past, the universe began to exist.

Everything is a Mess

I lived in two apartments in a row in buildings with terrible water heaters. Every time I stepped into the shower, I had to be ready to spin knobs at any moment, because the water would randomly go from scalding hot to ice cold at a moment's notice. And while I'm pretty sure it was the water heater's fault, it could have been a random low probability event of thermodynamics.

There are four thermodynamic laws, but here we are only concerned with the second one. It says that the entropy in any closed isolated system always, on average, increases. Everything eventually reaches what is known as thermal equilibrium, which is a state of maximum entropy, and then no further changes can be made. Entropy is a fancy term for disorder. The second law of thermodynamics is the reason that your room never cleaned itself when you were a child. It's the reason your bath water never suddenly becomes cold at one end of the tub and hot at the other (if you still take baths for some reason, you weirdo.)

The universe, by definition, contains everything. So it is, by definition, a closed system. Nothing outside it can act on it, because there is nothing outside it. So the second law of thermodynamics applies to the universe. It is headed for maximum entropy. It is becoming more and more disordered. When the entire universe reaches thermal equilibrium, it's what scientists refer to as "heat death." The universe, given sufficient time, will die.

So let's imagine for a moment that we had no evidence for the big bang. We had no idea whether the universe had a beginning or not. Basically, let's pretend the whole first part of this chapter doesn't exist. We would still have to conclude the universe hasn't been around forever, because of thermodynamics. Because the question naturally arises: If the universe is headed for heat death, and the universe has been around forever, why isn't it dead? A quick look into the sky will confirm that the universe is very much not dead. Stars are pretty hot. Even the vacuum of space, though pretty cold, is not at absolute zero. There's heat out there. Once again, a lot of scientists realized this, and tried to come up with solutions for it.

1. *Back to the Bounces*

The oscillating model proposed in the 1960s was meant to solve the entropy problem as well. If the universe expands and contracts forever, it would never reach a final state of equilibrium. But in order for the math on this model to work, the oscillations have to increase with each cycle, and as a result, entropy is conserved. It isn't reset, so the problem remains. Again, that's in addition to all the problems with this theory we just talked about.

2. *The Hollywood Re-boot*

Inevitably, at some point in any sci-fi franchise, a new director is given the helm who hates everything the previous one did. In order to erase everything, the most common mechanism used is the wormhole. Just send all the characters through a magical space tunnel to an alternate universe where none of that other stuff happened, and you're good to go. Re-boot complete.

Cosmologists entertained the idea that black holes could spawn wormholes. Bubbles of "false vacuum" energy could tunnel through these, and spawn a new universe on the other side, which would be closed off from us in this universe when the wormhole closed.

The concept of a "vacuum" has been changed a lot recently. Vacuums aren't empty. They have properties, and those properties determine the kinds of particles that exist in them. The lowest energy vacuum is called a "true vacuum" and it's what we live in.

It's the one with four separate basic forces. It is suspected that there are two other kinds of vacua. In the electroweak vacuum, the electromagnetic force and the weak force are combined. In this type of vacuum there is no chemistry because electrons don't attach to nuclei. In the grand-unified vacuum, the electromagnetic force, the weak force, and the strong force are all one force. These types of vacua (if they exist) have much higher energy content than true vacuum. The high energy makes them unstable, and they quickly "decay" into true vacuum. Due to the law of the conservation of energy, all the stored energy has to go somewhere. It is released as a hot fireball of particles.

It is by this mechanism that scientists thought wormholes could spawn a new universe. In fact, the theory was a bet between Steven Hawking and James Preskill, which Hawking admitted he lost in 2004, because it would require that information could be lost forever by escaping to another universe. But quantum theory requires information be preserved in black holes, both when they form and when they evaporate. But this wasn't the only attempt to find a mechanism for multiple universes.

3. *The red pill was just acid.*

Some scientists then hypothesized that false vacuum is dominant in the universe. This goes back to Inflationary Theory mentioned before. According to one version of the theory, our universe used to be all false vacuum. If conditions were just so, the false vacuum would inflate so quickly that the decay would turn into bubbles. In other words, as it decays into true vacuum, even though the true vacuum expands, it doesn't expand as fast as the false vacuum. These bubbles of true vacuum, viewed from observers inside them, would appear open and infinite, even though they are finite, and new bubbles would constantly form in the expanding sea of false vacuum.

The solution proposed was that, inevitably, some of these bubbles would form in a state of thermal disequilibrium. If you have enough bedrooms, one of them will eventually get a gust of wind that cleans it for you. We find ourselves in such a universe, and of course we do because it is the only kind of universe that could support our existence.

Here's the problem. In inflationary cosmology, there are two ways in which an ordered state capable of supporting observers could form. One is by being part of a young world that has not yet reached thermal equilibrium. The second way is a thermal fluctuation in an older world that has reached equilibrium. A thermal fluctuation is a just a quick moment of random disorder (like the random change of temperature in my shower.) Since the vacuum is expanding, the newer bubbles of true vacuum in the expansion will be very small compared to the older ones. Therefore, disordered states that are at or near thermal equilibrium should strongly dominate the landscape. So observers are far more likely to exist in a state of thermal fluctuation than in a new bubble. The problem is the thermal fluctuation should be really small too.

A physicist named Roger Penrose figured out the odds of an area the size of our observable universe coming into existence via a thermal fluctuation. The number he came up with was one part in $10^{10^{(123)}}$.[7] To put that into perspective, the odds of our entire solar system being formed instantly by random collisions of particles is one part in $10^{10^{(60)}}$, which is insane, but almost reasonable in comparison to $10^{10^{(123)}}$.[8] It is incomprehensibly more likely that every shower in every bathroom in the world would turn cold at the exact same time as mine due to a thermal fluctuation.

---

[7]   Roger Penrose, "Time-Asymmetry and Quantum Gravity" in *Quantum Gravity 2*, ed. C.J. Ishim, R. Penrose, and D.W. Sciama (Oxford: Clarendon, 1981), 249.

[8]   William Lane Craig, "Reasonable Faith", 148.

The most likely scenario in this case is that the universe is the size of your brain. A thermal fluctuation resulted in your brain, and everything around you is an illusion. You are in the matrix, but the red pill is just an acid trip. There is no outside. Your own body doesn't exist. This book doesn't exist. Nothing exists.

A physicist in the 1800s named Ludwig Boltzmann offered a similar hypothesis. While inflationary cosmology wasn't a concept yet, he still offered that maybe the universe as a whole had indeed reached heat death, and what we saw was simply a thermal fluctuation. Inflationary cosmology, though more complicated, runs into essentially the same problem. It has become known as the invasion of the Boltzmann brains. These brains would be far more plentiful than actual observers in the inflationary multiverse, so each of us, if we accept this as an explanation for our observed low entropy, are rationally obligated to regard everything around us as an illusion.

Getting to the Point

Okay, this is getting weird. But that's okay. That's the point. The point about the point in the past that started it all. The reason the universe is in a state of disequilibrium is that the universe hasn't existed forever. Heat death is inevitable, but it's not here now, because the universe has only existed for a finite amount of time. It had a beginning. And my water heater just sucks.

CHAPTER 5

HELLO, GOD?

Modus Ponens:

1. If a, then b.
2. a.
3. Therefore, b.

If the premises can be proved more plausible than their negations, the conclusion necessarily follows.

1. Everything that begins to exist has a cause.
2. The universe began to exist.
3. Therefore, the universe has a cause.

The cosmological argument is a modus ponens. Premise one is true. Premise two is true. Philosophy proves it. Cosmology proves it. Thermodynamics proves it. The conclusion, then, is true.

Conclusion: The universe has a cause.

Some people have accepted the two premises, but still deny the conclusion. Here's a couple reasons.

Some say the cosmological argument is guilty of the fallacy of equivocation. This is an informal logical fallacy where a word with more than one meaning is used twice in an argument, and the meanings aren't the same. A common example goes like this:

1. A feather is light.
2. Whatever is light is not dark.
3. A feather is not dark.

Here light is used twice and means two different things, so the argument is invalid. Objectors to the cosmological argument say that the equivocation fallacy is committed with the word "cause." They say "cause" in premise one means, "something that transforms previously existing materials from one state to another." But in the conclusion, cause means "something that creates an effect out of nothing." Therefore the argument is invalid.

But cause means the same thing in both statements. It means "something that produces effects." This is simpler than either definition presented above, and it works. The argument is not guilty of the fallacy of equivocation.

Others argue that the argument is valid, but that there is no reason to assume there is only one cause. This is technically true. The argument does not prove a single cause of the universe. There could be multiple causes. But Occam's Razor would compel us to stick with a singular cause. Occam's Razor states that, given competing theories, and all other things being equal, one should go with the simplest explanation. So until any evidence for multiple causes presents itself, I'm sticking with just one.

A final, less common objection is that a first cause is incomprehensible. It is surprising to me that this objection isn't brought up more often, because it was the only one that I thought had a good point. It goes like this: The cause of the Big Bang cannot be *after* the Big Bang, because backward causation is impossible. Neither can the cause of the Big Bang be *before* the Big Bang, since the singularity constitutes the beginning of time. Therefore, the universe cannot have a cause.

I think this objection is valid, but it is also a false dilemma, and so we can solve it by presenting a third option. Why can't the cause of the Big Bang be simultaneous with it? Indeed, when we examine what the nature of the first cause must be, we find that this is probably the case.

The universe contains all matter, all energy, all space, and all time. The singularity is the beginning of the universe. The cause of all space and time must then exist outside of space and time. It must be timeless and spaceless. Because it is timeless, it must be changeless, because change must occur in time. It can't be material either, because the universe contains all material. Because it is timeless, it has no beginning and no cause.

Finally, as Dr. William Craig points out, the cause must be *personal.* The beginning of the universe cannot have a scientific explanation, since there is no before, and therefore there are no scientific laws. So the only other explanation is that an agent *decided* to create the universe. Not only that, but there are only two things that can be called timeless and immaterial. Disembodied minds and abstract objects. But by the very definition of an abstract object, it doesn't cause anything. Numbers are a common example of abstract objects. So the number three, for example, never caused anything to happen. That leaves a disembodied mind. A mind that decided, timelessly, to create a universe. It is meaningless to ask what the mind was doing before creating the universe, because there was no time before the universe. It certainly existed, but in a timeless and changeless state. The mind choosing to create doesn't necessitate that it change either. It could simply timelessly intend to create the universe, and do so.

This timeless, spaceless, immaterial, personal, omnipotent mind sounds a lot to me like what most people refer to as God. If you prefer to call it something else, feel free to do so. I won't try to stop you. Call it "SuperMind" or "Chad." The point is, whatever you call it, it definitely exists. And it created the universe. For the purposes of this book, I will be conforming to convention and referring to this entity as God.

CHAPTER 6

ANSWERS IN TIME

My mind formulated the problem as follows. The traditional view of God is that he is omniscient. If God is all knowing, then God knows every action I will ever take and every thought I will ever have. And if he knows that, then my freedom is an illusion. All free will is an illusion. Every action, and even worse, every thought, was determined at the foundation of time. My thoughts and actions may seem free, but they are not. This has several effects. First, it makes me no longer responsible for my actions. Second, it makes God responsible for everything. The Holocaust, the Crusades, AIDS, cancer, abortion, rape, etc. All of it is God's will. Every terrible thing that has happened in your life was not only foreknown by God, but caused by him as well. This not only applies to human action, but to natural evil, like sickness, disease, and decay. Pain came from God. Evil came from God. God is evil. His perfect knowledge of all things past, present, and future, lines up perfectly with Isaac Newton's deterministic world. Nothing could be other than what it is. Third, it makes the very thing that defines my humanity an illusion. If I do not have the ability to make moral choices, I am an intelligent animal. Nothing more.

And I found out pretty fast that I wasn't the first one to reason this way. The famous Thomas Aquinas said as much.

To him, the cause of all things is God's knowledge. There is no distinction between what God causes and what he permits. There is only what he knows. Aquinas allows a sense of divine permission, when dealing with the problem of evil, but only allows it because he says that God cannot be evil. These statements are contradictory.

This is the point where I started my journey. It was a bleak starting point to say the least. I first thought that maybe God doesn't exist at all, but as we have seen, he most certainly does. So I was back to where I started. Is God evil? Is he a moral monster? What I found out was that in order to answer this question, I had to study something that, on the surface, seems almost completely unrelated: the nature of time. The problem of pain and evil and the nature of time are intrinsically related. To solve the former, we must first understand the later. And just as with the question of God's existence, we start with Einstein.

Relativity for Dummies

A lot of people don't realize that relativity theory is composed of two different theories. Special Relativity Theory, or STR, is a theory of time applicable to objects in constant motion. Einstein attempted to apply STR to accelerating and decelerating objects, and ended up instead creating a new theory of gravity, which is called the General Theory of Relativity, or GTR. Both theories have been repeatedly empirically verified, and are almost definitely true. In our discussion of time, we will mostly be concerned with STR, which isn't as hard to get a basic understanding of as you might think.

Galileo and Newton

People had some idea of the concepts of relativity long before Einstein. Galileo provided a pretty good explanation of the idea in the 1600s, and it's worth re-printing here.

Shut yourself up with some friend in the main cabin below decks on some large ship, and have with you there some flies, butterflies, and other small flying animals. Have a large bowl of water with some fish in it; hang up a bottle that empties drop by drop into a wide vessel beneath it.

With the ship standing still, observe carefully how the little animals fly with equal speed to all sides of the cabin.

The fish swim indifferently in all directions; the drops fall into the vessel beneath; and, in throwing something to your friend, you need to throw it no more strongly in one direction than another, the distances being equal; jumping with your feet together, you pass equal spaces in every direction.

When you have observed all of these things carefully (though there is no doubt that when the ship is standing still everything must happen this way), have the ship proceed with any speed you like, so long as the motion is uniform and not fluctuating this way and that.

You will discover not the least change in all the effects named, nor could you tell from any of them whether the ship was moving or standing still.

In jumping, you will pass on the floor the same spaces as before, nor will you make larger jumps toward the stern than towards the prow even though the ship is moving quite rapidly, despite the fact that during the time that you are in the air the floor under you will be going in a direction opposite to your jump.

In throwing something to your companion, you will need no more force to get it to him whether he is in the direction of the bow or the stern, with yourself situated opposite.

The droplets will fall as before into the vessel beneath without dropping towards the stern, although while the drops are in the air the ship runs many spans.

The fish in the water will swim towards the front of their bowl with no more effort than toward the back, and will go with equal ease to bait placed anywhere around the edges of the bowl.

Finally the butterflies and flies will continue their flights indifferently toward every side, nor will it ever happen that they are concentrated toward the stern, as if tired out from keeping up with the course of the ship, from which they will have been separated during long intervals by keeping themselves in the air....

SAGREDUS:

Although it did not occur to me to put these observations to the test when I was voyaging, I am sure that they would take place in the way you describe.

In confirmation of this I remember having often found myself in my cabin wondering whether the ship was moving or standing still; and sometimes at a whim which I have supposed it going one way when its motion was the opposite....[9]

The inside of the ship is what is referred to as an inertial frame for the things inside it. As long as there is no acceleration or deceleration, motion inside the frame will be the same as if the ship were at rest. This is the reason why you'd still die in a

---

[9]   Galileo Galilei, "Dialogues Concerning the Two Chief World Systems" (February 1632)

free-falling elevator even if you jumped before it hit the ground. You reversed your motion relative to the inertial frame inside the elevator, but relative to the outside frame, you've subtracted only a tiny fraction of your speed as you plummet towards your death.

Newton mathematically described this version of relativity in his famous Principia, and it still applies today. He described, for example, how two asteroids could be in motion relative to each other, even though one of them is actually at rest in space. This is not difficult to imagine.

The big problem in physics by the end of the 1800s was to combine Newtonian mechanical theory with electrodynamic theory, which is the study of the electro-magnetic spectrum, which includes light. The reason this was a problem was that there was no such relativity in electrodynamics. Light is a wave, and like all waves, it has to move through something. For example, sound waves have to move through air. That's why in space, no one can hear you scream.

No one knew what substance it was the light moved though, so they called the mystery substance the "aether." Recall that the Doppler Effect is what causes waves to expand or contract based on the motion of the object emitting them. An important characteristic to understand about waves is that they always travel at the same speed regardless of the emitting source. If you stand on top of a car and throw a baseball, the baseball will have the velocity of your arm plus the velocity of the car. But if the car honks its horn and it's 59°F outside, the sound wave will travel at 761mph whether the car is traveling at 10 mph or 100 mph.

Once the speed of light had been firmly established, people quickly realized that it could be used to determine absolute motion. In other words, it could eliminate Galilean Relativity. If you measured the speed of light from different directions, you could figure out what direction and what speed you yourself were moving through the aether. If you were moving toward the source of light, the speed of light should be faster than if you are moving away from the source. If you measured the speed of light to be exactly 186,000 miles per second, you could correctly conclude that you are at rest in absolute space.

But this turned out not to be the case. Experiments failed to detect any motion of the earth through space, even though the earth is orbiting the sun. It's obviously moving, but the speed of light was the same no matter what direction they measured it from. An airplane can break the sound barrier if it travels fast enough, but no matter how fast it travels, it will never break the light barrier. If a rocket travelled at 99% of the speed of light and turned on a headlight, the pilot in the rocket and a guy off in the distance would measure the speed of the light from the headlight to be 186,000 miles per second. If the guy in the distance was moving towards the rocket at 99% of the speed of light, he would measure the speed of light from the headlight to be 186,000 miles per second. If the guy in the distance was moving away from the rocket at 99% of the speed of light, he would measure the speed of light from the headlight to be 186,000 miles per second. I know how repetitive this is sounding, but it's important to understand just how totally weird and contradictory this situation is. It doesn't make any sense, and defies the rules of basic arithmetic.

Lorentz and Einstein

The first guy to come up with a possible solution was a physicist named Hendrik A. Lorentz. He proposed the idea that maybe the measuring devices used to measure light's speed expanded and contracted, and clocks slowed down and sped up in proportion to the observer's motion through the aether. So the speed of light would always be measured the same, when in fact it was not. On this theory, absolute motion, absolute space, and absolute time exist, but can't be measured. He didn't just leave it as an idea either. He did the math, making a set of equations that you could use to correct for motion through the aether to make your measurements accurate.

Then in 1905, a guy no one had ever heard of named Albert Einstein proposed a different solution. Einstein was an empiricist. Empiricism is the philosophy that knowledge is composed only of sense experience, concepts, and propositions. And concepts and propositions get meaning only in their relation to sense experience. If you can't sense it, it's meaningless. The entire field of metaphysics is essentially thrown out the window. It's on this basis that he began his paper. The paper that changed the way we see the universe.

The Special Theory of Relativity

Okay, here we go. First things first: the "aether" is gone. It doesn't exist. It isn't necessary. Next, we define what "time" means. More specifically, we define what we mean when we say that two events are "simultaneous." Assume that the time required for light to travel from point A to point B is the same as the time required for light to travel from point B to point A. In other words, the one-way velocity of light is constant. Operating on this assumption, Einstein proposes we could pretty easily synchronize a clock located at point A with a clock located at point B. All we have to do is send a light signal from A to B, which will then reflect back to A. Point A knows what time it is when the signal leaves, and knows that time it is when the signal returns. So we know that the signal arrived at B half way between these two times. From this information, it is pretty easy to synchronize the clocks at point A and B. We can then call two events "simultaneous" if they occur at the same time on the two synchronized clocks.

Now here is where the theory goes from mind-numbingly boring to mind-blowing. With the aether gone, absolute space is gone too. And if absolute space goes, absolute motion and absolute rest necessarily go with it. Bodies are therefore in motion or at rest only in relation to each other. There is no reference frame. The question of whether an object is actually moving or not, just became utterly meaningless.

Now imagine that that rocket ship from earlier is passing by the earth on its way to some other planet. It's still traveling at 99% of the speed of light. Let's also say that the rocket ship and the earth have synchronized clocks. Also, for the purposes of this scenario, the earth has a giant headlight on it. Now let's say that when the rocket ship is directly abeam the earth, they both turn on their headlights at the same time. Remember, light is a wave, and it travels at the same speed regardless of how fast the source is moving. That means that the two light beams will reach the planet in the distance at the same time. But, while the light was in transit, the rocket ship got a lot closer to the other planet, while the earth did not. That means the rocket ship will receive the return signal much sooner, but since the speed of light is the same in all inertial frames, the rocket ship detects no velocity for itself. Remember that the rocket ship and the earth have no absolute velocity. So when the guy on the rocket ship and the guy on the earth divide the travel time of the signal in half, they will get vastly different answers for when the signal reached the planet. Again, there is no absolute motion. It is just as accurate to say that the distant planet is approaching the rocket ship, and that the earth is traveling away from it. So whose answer is right? When did the light signals reach the distant planet? It seems that they arrived at different times, simultaneously.

To which Einstein would reply, "Yep." The result of abandoning absolute space is that the word "simultaneous" becomes relative to motion. As a direct result, time itself becomes relative to motion. Events that are simultaneous to one guy and in one place moving at a certain speed are not simultaneous to a different guy in a different place moving at a different speed. And neither guy is correct. And both guys are correct. What's more, something that hasn't happened yet for guy A, might have already happened for guy B, and both of those statements are accurate and true. The question of what time the event "actually" happened is meaningless.

As crazy as this is, without it, the GPS on your cellphone wouldn't work. The satellites it uses to triangulate your position when you are trying to find the nearest place that sells hot dogs has to compensate for motion and the resulting time dilation. We live in a relative world.

Omniscience Just Got Complicated

So the question then arises, which time frame is God in? There is no universal time. No reference frame is more privileged than any other. And there is an indefinite number of timeframes. So no matter which one God is in, he is no longer omniscient. He can only know the events in his own inertial frame. What's more, since God is an immaterial mind and not an object in motion, any selection of a time frame would be entirely arbitrary. He is also no longer omnipotent, because it would be impossible to sustain or cause events in any time frame other than his own.

One might suggest at this point that God is simply in every inertial timeframe. But this would not only take away God's omniscience, but it would make him thoroughly and cripplingly confused all the time. He would have an indefinite number of split consciousness, all completely isolated from each other.

In the next chapter, I'll explain the most common solution to this problem. It's the view held by the majority of the great philosophers and theologians throughout history, and it's held up remarkably well in the face of modern cosmology and relativity theory.

CHAPTER 7

GOD: THE STANDARD MODEL

Minkowski's SpaceTime

Reality under STR is fragmented. For any two objects to co-exist, they must be present at the same time, and therefore must be stationary. Here's why. Let's say we have object A and object B, and let's say they are some random distance apart and are in motion relative to each other (which, remember, is the only kind of motion there is.) Now let's say an event happens at A and another event happens at B. Now let's say that in A's inertial frame, the event at A and the event at B are simultaneous. Inherently, this means that in B's inertial frame, the event at A and the event at B are *not* simultaneous. The events therefore *cannot exist at the same time.* Under STR, no object can ever co-exist with a moving object. The only way A and B can exist at the same time is if they are at rest relative to each other. So once again we arrive at the hypothesis that everything, or at least nearly everything, is an illusion. If anything is in motion, it cannot co-exist with you.

What's more, any time I change my motion in any way, reality literally changes. The people I walk by on the sidewalk are experiencing a completely different reality than my own, and both are very real. Over extreme distances, the difference becomes literally significant. And if the motion becomes faster, the distance doesn't need to be that large for the differences to become significant. Even at a distance of the diameter of the earth, in the span of a tenth of a second, something could have literally happened in one country and literally not have happened yet in another.

Special Relativity was proposed in 1905, and people quickly began to uncover these dilemmas. How are we to respond to such obviously contradictory statements about how reality really is? By 1908, a German mathematician named Hermann Minkowski had proposed an answer. And as the theory of special relativity itself, it was a game changer. It fundamentally shifted how we view the universe. Minkowski proposed that reality does not consist of three-dimensional objects moving through time, but simply as a collection of *four-dimensional* objects that just exist. Since we can only apprehend three dimensions, we can't picture what four-dimensional objects look like, but we can still represent them mathematically.

When reality is viewed in this way, relativity disappears. Measurements of space and time are relative, but measurements of spacetime are absolute. Our entire life is a four-dimensional object that exists on a spacetime curve. (In the mathematics of spacetime, a curved path through space is the shortest.) The universe simply exists. It includes all of space and all of time, and it simply is. There is no past, present, nor future. There are simply events located in spacetime at certain points. They are all equally real. Events are simultaneous if they are both located in whatever "slice" of spacetime I happen to be looking at.

Minkowski's spacetime also explains why objects seemed to shrink or slow down when in motion. Those objects are actually four dimensional, and the shrinking and slowing is simply the result of viewing the four dimensional object from a different angle.

Simply put, Minkowski's spacetime provided an explanation for the brute facts put forth by relativity theory, and has since been largely accepted as the preferred view of reality in physics. Temporal becoming is an illusion. Our lives are spacetime curves. They never were and they never will be. They simply are.

Divine Timelessness

The obvious solution to the relationship between God and time would seem then to be that he is not located in spacetime. Indeed, why would he be? He created spacetime. The universe is an object that God made. The past, the present, and the future are all equally real to him. He is omniscient because he can view spacetime as a whole from the outside, while we are not simply due to the fact that we are located inside the universe. When we say that "God knows I will eat leftover pizza tonight," we mean that God can see the point on my "world line," as they are referred to, where I'm too lazy to make dinner and decide to eat leftover pizza. That action doesn't exist in the future. It simply exists as a point on a four-dimensional object. In a quick summary statement, God is timeless.

This position is further supported by a philosophical stance completely apart from relativity theory. God must be timeless because God is perfect, and existing in time is less perfect than existence in a timeless state. If the past is literally gone forever and the future literally does not exist yet, then a temporal being cannot possess it. Even a perfect memory isn't as good as an actual access to the past. Even perfect foreknowledge is not as good as really possessing the future. But God, being perfect, simply exists. He does not experience the loss of the past or the gain of the future. He simply possesses all of time at once, just has he possesses all of space.

God: The Standard Model

Unless, therefore, we obtain not simply determination of will, which is freely turned in this direction and that, and has its place amongst those natural goods which a bad man may use badly; but also a good will, which has its place among those goods of which it is impossible to make a bad use – unless the impossibility is given to us from God, I know not how to defend what is said: "What hast thou that thou didst not receive?" For if we have from God a certain free will, which may still be either good or bad: but the good will comes from ourselves; then that which comes from ourselves is better than that which comes from Him. But inasmuch as it is the height of absurdity to say this, they ought to acknowledge that we attain from God even a good will.[10] – Augustine

This is the doctrine of efficacious grace. Basically, God's grace is the one and only thing that can bring a person to salvation. Free will lost the capability to will to desire God when man first fell into sin. We, though "free" in a sense, cannot choose God. God chooses those who are pre-destined to be chosen. Put in more modern terms, God created your world line in spacetime. Some of those world lines end in eternal (or timeless) life. Others do not, to put it delicately. God doesn't direct or control the future.

---

[10] Augustine *A Treatise on the Merits and Forgiveness of Sins, and on the Baptism of Infants* 2.30 (in *Augustine, The Anti-Pelagian Writings,* trans. Peter Holmes; vol. V of *Select Library of the Nicene and Post-Nicene Fathers,* ed. Philip Schaff [Grand Rapids, Mich.: Eerdmans, 1971] p. 56)

He simply created all time when he created the universe, and it is as it is.

To be fair, not everyone who holds the view of divine timelessness also holds to the view of pre-destination. This is known as compatibilism. It is the view that God can "cause" future evil events simply by "allowing" them to happen. Human free will is not an illusion. The problem is in our understanding of free will. The medieval philosopher Anselm presented this view pretty well. He starts by defining free will. I should note here that Anselm is not known for being concise or easy to follow. This summary will be really brief and really rough, but for our purposes, it'll do. I'll italicize stuff that is really important. Ok, here we go.

Anselm Attempts to Reconcile

Anselm defines free will not as the ability to choose to sin or not to sin, for if this were true, he reasons, then God would not have free will. Sin is indecent and inexpedient, and makes one less free. Both man and angel had the ability to sin in the beginning, and did indeed do so. How then, can we say that they sinned by free will? And if they did not sin by free will, it would seem that they sinned necessarily. But if they sinned willingly, how so except by free will? The first angel and man had a free will that could not be coerced to sin, so they sinned completely willingly.

How then, is free will maintained after one has been made a slave to sin? Sin does not annul natural free will, but the use of free will now requires grace. Human free will originally had a "right nature" but lost it with the fall of man into sin. As long as the will has this right nature, it can preserve it. But how can it preserve it once it is lost? Once the right nature is lost, there is no free will capable of preserving it.

Even if the right nature of the will is absent, the natural power is still there. If you showed someone with perfect vision a mountain but there was no light, or something blocking his view, he would not see it, though his vision is perfect. The power of seeing the mountain, says Anselm, is in four things: in the one seeing, in the thing being seen, in what helps, and in what does not impede. In the same way, when we lose the right nature of the will, we do not lose the ability of will, but simply a factor. Freedom of will consists in reason and will. No one can be deprived of the right nature of the will except by his own choice. *Temptation can never overpower the will, but only make the task of willing difficult.* Even God cannot take free will. Will is the rectitude for justice. If God were to remove it, he would remove a rectitude. God would be removing the very will which he desires one to will. This is a clear contradiction.

After Anselm establishes what the will is, he attempts to reconcile it with divine foreknowledge. *God's foreknowledge must exist for there to be future things*, he says. Free choice must exist for there to be things that exist not by necessity. Therefore, they must coexist. God must foreknow even the free choices of men, knowing that they will be chosen freely. We often say something is necessary, not because it is compelled by some force, but simply because it is not impeded by anything. For example, we may say that God is necessarily immortal not because anything forces Him to be immortal, but because nothing can cause Him to not be immortal. Therefore, God's foreknowledge does not force one to sin or not to sin, but simply does not impede one's will to do this or that. He continues, simply saying that something is going to happen does not mean it happens by necessity. If one says, "A rebellion is going to take place tomorrow," it is still possible that it will not, even if it does. In this way, saying that God foreknows something does not mean that it cannot be freely chosen by a different agent. The will must operate freely, or it would not be operating at all. This means that sin must always be a free choice. If God's divine foreknowledge were to enforce necessity on all things he knows, than He Himself neither wills nor causes anything freely, but necessarily. There is no contradiction in saying that things can happen both by necessity and by free choice. Anselm likens this to perspective, where to one person, a man is departing, and to another in a different location, he is arriving. (Maybe Anselm influenced Einstein in writing STR? Probably not.)

Just as the temporal present includes all places and what is occurring in those places, the eternal present includes all time and what is occurring in those times. So when St. Paul says that God, foreknew, predestined, called, justified, and glorified His saints, none of these things happened before the others. Anselm says that whenever scripture speaks of things that involve free will as if they are necessary, it is referring to the eternal present, or events outside of time. My actions tomorrow do not exist now, but always exist in eternity. (Maybe Minkowski got his spacetime concept from Anselm? Probably not.)

So then does God know all things because they exist, or do they exist because He knows them? They can't owe their existence to God if he knows them because they exist. But if they exist because he knows them, then God sustains evil and unjustly punishes the wicked. Anselm says *we must then define evil as a lack of existence.* If we refer to good as righteousness, then unrighteousness is a lacking of righteousness, and is then nothing. But if we refer to good as benefit, then the opposite is affliction, which is accompanied by the very real thing: pain. Scripture confirms that God "brings peace and causes woes" (Isaiah 45:7).

Nothing has the power to will or move or act unless God bestows it. Anselm defines predestination as bringing about something to happen in the future. Whatever God declares will happen in the future must necessarily happen because God is truth. *As established earlier, nothing has the power to will or move or act unless God bestows it. Therefore God predestines our actions.* When God "hardens" people, he simply does not soften them. When he "leads them to temptation" he simply does not release them from it. In the same way, when God predestines evil people and evil acts, he simply does not aid in steering them to redemption. Therefore, according to Anselm, God can cause evil things not by compelling or constraining the will, but by leaving it to its own devices.

That is a very quick summary of the compatibilist view of free will and divine foreknowledge, from one of the greatest philosophers of all time. Not everyone agrees entirely with Anselm's take obviously, and I encourage you to explore various philosophers and their take on the issue of divine foreknowledge, free will, and evil. I believe you will find, as I did, that they are all pretty similar in the end. Now here's why they don't work.

Anselm Was Wrong

Let's start with Anselm's perspective analogy. He says things can happen by necessity and by free will in the same way that a man can be departing from one perspective and arriving from another. Why couldn't you use this same analogy to eliminate every contradiction ever? Maybe I can be married and be a bachelor in the same way that a man can be departing from one perspective and arriving from another. Maybe that shape can be a square and a circle in the same way that a man can be departing from one perspective and arriving from another. Obviously neither of those things can actually exist together. You can't eliminate inherent contradictions by likening them to a matter of perspective. He tries the same trick again when introducing the temporal and eternal perspectives, which is essentially the same thing as talking about existing inside or outside the spacetime continuum. Just because my perspective is temporal, or to update the phrase with Minkowski's spacetime, just because I can't see my entire world line, doesn't mean the entire world line doesn't exist. It does, and therefore so does my future, which cannot be changed. God created all of spacetime, the good and the evil. God is the cause. Free will is still an illusion.

Anselm says that when God "leads someone to temptation" he simply does not release them from it. When he predestines evil people and evil actions, he simply does not steer them toward redemption. But this is a clear contradiction to his earlier statement that the will is stronger than temptation in all cases. He says God can cause evil not by compelling or constraining the will, but by leaving it to its own devices, but what about his previously stated doctrine that nothing has the power to will or move unless God bestows it?

In short, Anselm is full of tricks of perspective, but they do nothing but dance around the problem, which still stands in all of its ugliness. God foreknows everything. God is outside of time. God created spacetime. God created evil. God caused all the evil in the world. God is responsible for evil. Free will is an illusion. God is evil.

The Counterfactuals of Eating Cake

A few hundred years after Anselm, another, and in my mind much better, famous attempt was made to harmonize human libertarian freedom with God's foreknowledge. It's known as Molinism, named after its founder: Luis de Molina, and it's the strongest attempt made in philosophy to have your cake and eat it too. Molinism is based on the concept of God's "middle knowledge" and "counterfactuals." A counterfactual is a conditional statement of unreality. It's a statement about how things could be rather than how they are, like "If I had bothered to study I would have passed the test," or "If they had Xbox in medieval times, Anselm wouldn't have written so much."

Molina said that God has three kinds of knowledge. Natural knowledge is the knowledge of all necessary truths. It includes stuff like 2+2=4, and all the possible worlds God could create. This knowledge is logically prior to God's decision to create the universe. Free knowledge is God's knowledge of all the truths of the world he did create. It includes stuff like "Pearl Harbor will be attacked on December 7, 1941" and "a hydrogen atom is composed of one proton and one electron." You could say that natural knowledge is knowledge of what *could* be and free knowledge is knowledge of what *will* be. Finally, middle knowledge is God's knowledge of what *would* be. In other words, middle knowledge is God's knowledge of counterfactuals. God knows, for example, that if you hadn't bought this book, I would be about five dollars poorer than I am. Molina claimed that God's middle knowledge is logically subsequent to his natural knowledge but prior to his free knowledge. In other words, God knew all counterfactuals before creating the universe. God's natural knowledge gave him a range of possible universes to create. His middle knowledge then gave him a subset of feasible worlds out of all the possible worlds. Out of that subset, he created the universe we live in.

By organizing God's knowledge in such a way, human freedom is said to be preserved. Before God created the universe, he looked at every universe that contained free creatures and all of their decisions that they would choose to make throughout all of time, then chose the one that fit his purposes. The molinist argues that just because God knows that an event will happen doesn't mean that it happens by necessity (similar to Anselm's analogy of the rebellion tomorrow.) Rather God can know the future choices of free agents because he simply chose to create a universe where agents would freely choose to do the things in God's divine plan. A comparison can be drawn from every day experience. Say a friend of yours, let's call him Gary, gets the exact same order at a restaurant every time you eat there. You meet as usual and sure enough, Gary orders the same sandwich, just like you thought he would. Obviously, just because you knew he would order it doesn't make his decision to do so compelled by you somehow. It was still a free choice on Gary's part.

This analogy is fallacious though, due to the brute fact that we human beings are *not* omniscient. The reason Gary is free to order a different sandwich is because it's possible that you are wrong. But God *is* omniscient. He can't be wrong. He sees all of spacetime, and he can't and does not make mistakes. The molinist would say that, if Gary had gotten a different sandwich, then God would have known that instead, and I would agree. God is omniscient in all possible worlds. That includes this one, and in this one, God knows that Gary will order that sandwich, and God can't be wrong. Gary's going to order that sandwich. Molina can't change the perspective to get around a contradiction any more than Anselm could. In other words, for an omnipotent being, there is no difference between certainty and necessity.

Also, the question arises, what grounds the eternal settledness of future free acts? It can't be because God wills them to exist, because then we are back to Anselm and determinism. And an agent can't will counterfactuals about himself, because they are by definition contrary to what the agent actually wills. They are what the agent would have done in a different possible world. So we are left to assume that, from all eternity, what a free agent would do in every possible scenario is simply there without reason. This would mean that the settledness of every possible world is an uncreated reality that coexists alongside God, which cannot be, because God created everything. And if you say that God created the counterfactuals, then you arrive back at determinism.

An even bigger problem with Molinism, I think, is a misconception of freedom. In order for someone to have freedom, it must be within his power to do otherwise, given the same set of conditions. Molinism denies this, saying that given a set of conditions, someone would behave as such, and God knows this. (Note: This is the standard "libertarian" definition of free will. There are competing definitions, but to enter into this realm would lead me too far astray. Libertarian free will is what us laymen naturally assume, in any case. For a thorough and solid defense of libertarian free will, I recommend "Mind, Brain, and Free Will" by Richard Swinburne.)

There is one more problem with Molinism, and classic pre-destination for that matter, and it's huge. But it'll take some time to get there. We have a lot more to talk about regarding time.

CHAPTER 8

THE PHOTON TWINS

At no time then hadst Thou not made any thing, because time itself Thou madest. And no times are coeternal with Thee, because Thou abidest; but if they abode, they should not be times. For what is time? Who can readily and briefly explain this? Who can even in thought comprehend it, so as to utter a word about it? But what in discourse do we mention more familiarly and knowingly, than time? And, we understand, when we speak of it; we understand also, when we hear it spoken of by another. What then is time? If no one asks me, I know: if I wish to explain it to one that asketh, I know not. – The Confessions of St. Augustine

So, God definitely exists. We know that, and there's no getting around it. He created the universe, which is everything that exists. The universe is all of spacetime, and that includes evil. Lots and lots of evil. Which God created. That's where our reasoning has led us. If it's solid, then that's the end, and I'd probably kill myself. But you will note, astute reader, that I have not killed myself, and am instead writing a book. So have hope, because our reasoning did have a flaw. So who got it wrong? It may surprise you to find that I think it was Minkowski.

Minkowski's spacetime is basically taken for granted in modern physics. Of all the things to challenge, why this? I think Minkowski spacetime is a lot like Infinite Set Theory mentioned before, in that it is very useful as a mathematical construct, but doesn't translate to the way things really are. For the next two chapters of this book, what I will essentially be presenting is a summary of Dr. William Craig's thesis on God's relationship to time, which was instrumental in my journey towards truth. His academic work was able to take what was a vague idea in my own mind and give it teeth, and I owe him a debt of gratitude. By the end of this book, my views will have parted ways with the great philosopher (and in fact, they already have; Dr. Craig is a Molinist), but I still have nothing but the utmost respect for him and his work, which he goes to tremendous lengths to make accessible to people like me.

So onward we press. To refresh, God is real. STR theory is true, and according to the theory as it is, if God exists within time, then he either exists in one reference frame or in a plurality of reference frames, most likely all of them. But if he is in one reference frame only, he is far from omniscient. And if he is in all reference frames, his consciousness is infinitely divided, and he is thoroughly confused all the time. The logical conclusion is that God exists outside of time. God is timeless. This seems inherently implied by the cosmological argument for God's existence, too. If God created the universe, he created time, and so there would be no reason he would be bound to time. The Minkowski interpretation of STR seems to confirm this. God simply created four dimensional spacetime (or maybe eleven dimensional spacetime if string theory turns out to be correct.) And if God is indeed outside of time, God is evil (though Dr. Craig would disagree with that statement). But if Minkowski was wrong, then reality becomes infinitely fragmented. What are we to make of this?

Back to Newton

Isaac Newton believed that time would exist without events. In other words, in a completely empty universe where nothing ever happened, time would still literally pass. (I'm not sure he was right on that, but for my purposes here it doesn't matter.) He believed that time was distinct from how we measure it. Newton also believed in the existence of God, and that God existed in this time, distinct from any measurements, which he referred to as "absolute time." To him, infinite time and infinite space must necessarily exist because God exists everywhere all the time.

Newton was unaware that the universe had a beginning or that time was relative to motion. He assumed that an ideal clock would measure time accurately. We now know that this isn't the case. Measuring any "absolute time" is impossible, because according to STR, there is no such thing as "absolute rest", and a clock would have to be in such a state to read accurately.

The key, though, is that STR shows there is no way to *measure* absolute time. Einstein removed Newton's God and substituted an observer viewing events by light signals, which is what we all are. Remember, Einstein was a verificationist. Statements that cannot be verified through the senses were meaningless to him. His special theory of relativity is also a verificationist theory. He defines time and simultaneity by verifiable means. Many people assume that STR disproved absolute time and absolute space, when in fact, it *presupposed* that they do not exist. There is no way to detect them, so there is no reason to think that they are real.

At first glance it would seem that verificationism is a quite reasonable position to hold, but it is actually an outmoded view in modern science and philosophy. Holding such a view forces one to abandon most metaphysical, ethical, and even scientific statements as meaningless. Even worse, verificationism is self-refuting. The statement, "Only sentences which can in principle be empirically verified are meaningful" is not an empirically verifiable sentence and therefore is meaningless by its own standards. It is worth noting that most of modern physics, like quantum mechanics and cosmology, has a large metaphysical aspect, which is incompatible with verificationism.

In short, STR proves only that it is impossible for a finite observer, dependent on light signals for observation, to know that time it actually is. It leaves the question of whether such an absolute time exists, open.

Thank Goodness the Moon Was There When We Landed

Recall that Einstein and Minkowski weren't the only ones to deal with relativity. Hendrik Lorentz took a crack at it too, with the hypothesis that measuring devices shrink in the direction of their motion through the aether. The faster you move, the more the device contracts, causing the measured speed of light to stay the same. In the same way, clocks slow down when they move through the aether. He wrote equations to show how to correct for these errors, and they became the core of Einstein's special relativity theory. If we follow Lorentz, Einstein's clock synchronization would only work in the reference frame of absolute time.

Lorentz's and Einstein's relativity interpretations are empirically equivalent. Lorentz has been the quiet kid in the corner when it comes to relativity, but he's there. And recently, people have started to pay attention to him again. In fact the first hint that Lorentz might be right came in the 1960s, in what was called the EPR experiment, after the three men who devised it: Einstein, Boris Podolsky, and Nathan Rosen. In order to understand the experiment, we'll need a very brief and entirely inadequate summary of quantum theory.

At the beginning of the twentieth century, two guys proposed two hypotheses that fit neatly with each other, and defied the rest of physics. Max Plank proposed that electrons radiate energy in stages or "quanta" randomly and without cause. He did this to solve a problem in classical physics called the "ultraviolet catastrophe" that predicted that every object would instantaneously lose its heat by radiating a burst of energy at frequencies beyond the ultraviolet range, which they obviously do not. Around the same time, Einstein proposed that light comes in compact lumps, which he named "photons" to explain a phenomenon called the "photoelectric effect." The problem was, light was a wave, and everybody knew it. Interference experiments had demonstrated as much.

A few years later a guy named Niels Bohr set out to explain why electrons don't just crash into the positively charged nucleus of the atom. According to the math, as an electron orbited, it should radiate all its energy in less than a millionth of a second and crash. Bohr adopted Plank's quanta for electron orbits, which established a smallest possible orbit, thus forbidding a crash. His theory matched the color spectrum of the elements perfectly. Then, a guy named Louis de Broglie proposed that if light had a particle and wave-like nature, maybe matter had a dual nature too. If one viewed the electron as a wave, he could derive Bohr's ad hoc theory about quantum electron orbits. Over the next few years, the dual nature of matter as a particle and a wave became more widely accepted, and another guy named Erwin Schrodinger wrote an equation to describe a piece of matter's "wave function."

Every particle has a wave function, which describes the probability of finding the particle in a particular place. Here's where it gets weird: a wave function describes the *objective* probability of *finding* a particle in a place. It's not as if it is somewhere before being observed and we just can't be sure where. Before a particle is observed, it is literally a wave, which can be proven by running a classic interference experiment often done in particle physics. Quantum theory says the observation itself causes the wave function to "collapse" producing the particle. In other words, unobserved particles are waves. What is meant exactly by "observation" is still debated.

For all practical purposes, quantum theory is proven correct. Its implications however, are a huge topic of debate in physics and philosophy circles, and have been since the theory's inception. Bohr took quantum theory at face value. Einstein was less convinced, insisting that nothing is characterized by indeterminacy, no matter how small, and quantum theory applies to matter of all sizes anyway. To quote him, "I think that a particle must have a separate reality independent of the measurements. That is, an electron has spin, location, and so forth even when it is not being measured. I like to think the moon is there even if I am not looking at it."

So the EPR team came up with a thought experiment involving polarized light. Light's electric field can point in any direction perpendicular to the direction the light is traveling. We call the direction of a beam of light's electric field its "polarization." Polarized sunglasses work by only allowing light polarized in certain directions to pass through. If an atom is raised to a certain excited state, it will return to its ground state by two quantum jumps in succession, releasing two photons that always travel in opposite directions and always display the same polarization as each other. These are called "twin state photons." So let's say we put two detectors in opposite directions to detect these two photons, with detector B slightly further away from the source than detector A. Since the photons are traveling away from the atom at the speed of light in opposite directions, they are separating from each other at twice the speed of light. There is no way for them to physically affect each other. Quantum theory says no property is physically real until observed. That includes polarization. Since the atom is unchanged, it cannot be considered to have "observed" the two photons. Therefore, they do not have any polarization, much less the same polarization, until observed by the detectors. This means that before the photon was detected by detector A, neither photon was polarized at all. But as soon as photon A is detected, photon B takes on the same polarization as photon A. But remember, they were separating at twice the speed of light, so it was impossible for photon A to effect photon B. Yet because of detector A, it is possible to know photon B's polarization without observing it.

When this very test was finally run in 1964, it turned out that Bohr was right. One particle had a polarization when it was measured, and the other particle took on the same polarization without any mechanical interaction. There are only two explanations: either there are influences that can travel faster than light or the particles are non-causally correlated so that both take on certain properties instantaneously. In either case, we have to sacrifice the definition of simultaneity from STR.

Then, scientists discovered what the preferred reference frame might be. In 1965, the cosmic background radiation predicted by the Big Bang Theory was detected, and recently, tests have detected the earth's motion relative to it. The background radiation is a rest relative to space. The absolute motion that couldn't be detected from the visible light spectrum has been detected in the microwave spectrum. This isn't to say that there is an actual substance through which light moves. Light is a particle wave that travels through empty space just fine. It is only to say that Lorentz was onto something.

GTR

Again, none of this means that STR is wrong or that we need to give up any of the mathematics it describes. It only means we need to interpret the math differently. Not only that, but remember that STR deals only with uniform motion. To deal with acceleration and deceleration, Einstein crafted his General Theory of Relativity (GTR.) Einstein's goal was to equate non-inertial frames with the inertial frames of STR. When formulating his General Theory, Einstein started with the observation that the effects of acceleration and the effects of gravity were similar. This is why, for example, when a pilot rolls into a sixty degree bank, which is an acceleration around a curve, and he is pressed back into his seat, we refer him feeling the force of "two Gs." He is feeling the force of twice the normal gravitational pull of the earth.

Einstein proposed that we view gravity not as a force acting at a particular distance but as an acceleration of objects through spacetime. An object warps spacetime like a ball resting on a sheet. So objects close to the ball would slide down the slope of the sheet toward it. This would be analogous to its gravitational pull. This is a two dimensional example of something that occurs in three dimensions, but Einstein worked out the mathematics and his work ended up replacing Newton's equations. But it's important to note that at the end of crafting GTR, acceleration and rotation remained distinct from uniform motion. GTR curved spacetime. If you introduce flatness into the equations, you arrive back at STR.

A nice thing that resulted from GTR was that it introduced a new cosmic perspective to STR, and even though Einstein's model of the universe was static, this "cosmic time" is applicable to an expanding universe as well. The local time of an observer at a fixed point in the expanding universe will coincide with cosmic time in his vicinity. Put simply, cosmic time in GTR is not tied to inertial frames. It is privileged in a way very similar to Newton's absolute time. It is not metaphysically necessary or independent of physical measurement like absolute time, but it keeps its privileged status, independent of motion.

Real Time

By rejecting Minkowski's interpretation of STR in favor of Lorentz, I've shown that the main argument for a static conception of time is flawed. Minkowski's interpretation is often referred to as the B-Theory of time, and it's very useful in physics. But that doesn't mean it is representative of the way things are. However, we haven't shown that Minkowski was wrong. Only that it's possible that he was wrong. We now have two competing interpretations of STR.

The dynamic theory of time, or A-theory, holds that space and time are significantly different. That they aren't all part of one four-dimensional super-shape called spacetime. A-theory says that time really passes, that the only thing that is real is the present. The past is literally gone forever and the future literally does not exist yet. So are there any good arguments that A-theory is right? What's more, so what if there are? What does that have to do with God? What does it have to do with the pain and injustice in my life and in the world?

Everything! Bear with me, dear reader. The answers will come in time.

CHAPTER 9

MINKOWSKI AND McTAGGART: NOT BFFS

It should be emphasized just how radical a re-interpretation of time it was that Minkowski proposed. B-theory makes time tenseless, and we experience tense every day. If Minkowski was right, we are stuck in a massive illusion every day from which there is no escape. Be forewarned, dear reader, that things are about to get weird. This will be the most difficult and abstract chapter in this book. But it's also a crucial link in the chain, and the destination will be worth it. So, the question before us is, "Does time really pass?" Or more accurately speaking "Is temporal becoming real?" It's time to find out.

My Properly Basic Burrito

Psychologist William Friedman says it succinctly: "The division between past, present, and future so deeply permeates our experience that it is hard to imagine its absence."[11] We all experience the true reality of the passage of time. We all

---

[11]   William Friedman, *About Time* (Cambridge, Mass.: MIT Press, 1990), 92.

instinctively believe that there is a real distinction between the future, the past, and the present. Our belief in the literal passage of time isn't even a rational attempt to explain our experience. It is what is known in philosophy as a "properly basic belief." A basic belief is a belief that is not based on other beliefs. For example, as I type this, there is a half-eaten burrito sitting on the table in front of me. It was really big and I couldn't finish it. When I look at it, I don't think to myself, "I am receiving visual stimuli causing a burrito to appear to be sitting on the table in front of me. The best explanation of this phenomenon is that there is an actual burrito on the table that is causing me to see it." Instead, I just form the belief, "There's a burrito on the table."

In fact, most beliefs we hold are basic beliefs. Everything you remember, everything you perceive through your senses, and everything you believe when someone tells you is a basic belief. The thing that makes the belief "properly" basic is the circumstances surrounding it. If I looked at the burrito and formed the belief "there is a cheeseburger on the table," the belief would not be properly basic for me. Some properly basic beliefs are held more strongly than others. The more strongly the belief is held, the more strong the evidence required to cause me to abandon it. If a properly basic belief is shown to be false, it is "defeated." If I left the room for a minute, I would still have a properly basic belief grounded in my memory that there is a burrito on the table, but if I got back and found that my sister had eaten it, my belief would be defeated.

Basically, what all this means is that you're justified in holding a properly basic belief until you encounter a defeater strong enough to cause you to abandon it. For a good example, refer back to the Boltzmann brains. It is impossible to prove that you are not a random fluctuation that resulted in a single brain, and that everything around you including your own past is not an illusion. But the mere possibility of that is not a strong enough defeater for your belief that the world is not an illusion. (At least I hope it's not.)

I would argue, along with Dr. Craig, that the passage of time is a properly basic belief, for a couple reasons. First, we experience events, and we experience them occurring in the present. Under the static view of time, we cannot experience the present, because there is no such thing as the present. Now granted, we are not always correct when we experience something occurring in the present, because our observation is limited by the speed of light. But just because we may see something that occurred in the past, we are still observing that thing in the present. The experience is still present to us. I am still "seeing" the event "now."

Second, and even more compelling I think, is that our attitude toward the past and the future is very different. If time is without tense, there is no reason to look at past events with fondness or with regret. Likewise there is no reason to anticipate or dread the future. We could with equal justification and rationality regret the future or anticipate the past. In fact it would be irrational to hold any of these attitudes toward the past or the future, since all events are equally real. Another interesting point is that we may rationally regard the same event differently depending on whether it is in the future or in the past. Take a test for example. A test for which you didn't prepare well. If it's in the future, you will rationally feel anxiety. But if you already took the test, you will rationally feel relief that it's over. If B-theory is right, there is no justification for this change. The event did not change tense. There is no tense. Your change in attitude would be entirely irrational and unmotivated. It would be the same as feeling a sense of relief that a gunman was standing on your right side instead of your left side.

Remember, according to Minkowski, time does not have a direction. Some scientists have attempted to give it one by appealing to various physical processes; the second law of thermodynamics for example. But according to B-theory, we could just as accurately call an increase in entropy "earlier than" the decrease. The choice is arbitrary.

In fact, A-theory is the only explanation of two aspects of time: "anisotropy" and "directionality." Isotropy is the property of being the same in all directions. Space is isotropic. The north and south poles of the earth are, for example, arbitrarily assigned. But time is anisotropic. It is defined by the "earlier than" direction and the "later than" direction. Events are ordered objectively as earlier than or later than other events. Time's "directionality" means it is oriented in one direction. A thing can have anisotropy without having directionality. Escalators can go up or down for example. But time always goes from the past to the future. If we are asked if the War of 1812 occurred before or after the Revolutionary War, we all say "after." Under B-theory, there is no explanation for time's anisotropy or directionality. But on A-theory, such properties are grounded. Under A-theory, time cannot lapse backwards. For an object to continue to exist, a moment must come into existence after the present moment. It is impossible that the next moment come into existence before the present moment, or we would be saying that the object endured from the present to the past. It makes no sense to say an object "continued" to exist from the present moment to a past moment.

In light of this, Minkowski's static time seems ridiculous to say the least, and you may be wondering why anyone would hold to it. Indeed, I think many people do simply because they believe Minkowski's interpretation of STR is the only one there is. But there are other arguments against A-theory, and we'll look at them now.

Chronons and the Tiny Stadium

One common argument is that if A-theory is correct, it is impossible to define the present, because the passage of time can't be explained. In order for A-theory to be correct, the passage of time can't just be in my mind. It must literally pass. But if time literally passes, questions that can't be answered result, the most common one being, "How fast does time flow?" We measure distance in units of time, miles per hour for example. But we can't measure time in units of distance. And we can't measure time in units of time. As your English teacher told you in middle school, you can't use a word in the definition. How fast does a minute pass? What answer can be given besides, "One minute"?

I think this problem can be solved though. When we talk about the flow of time, it is a metaphor for things becoming real. We aren't saying that a future event takes on a present tense. Rather we are saying that a thing literally comes into being in the present. An "event" is when a "thing" becomes real. Before that, the thing literally did not exist. This is a view called "presentism," and I'll go deeper into it in just a minute.

A more serious issue against the passage of time is defining exactly how long the "present" is. If only the present is real, then we can't say the present consists of this "instant". An instant in time is like a point in space. It has no dimensions. It only exists mathematically. Likewise, an instant has no duration. If something exists for only an instant, then it doesn't exist at all. Even worse, if time is composed of successive instants, then time cannot ever pass, because 0+0+0... equals 0.

One solution is to find a minimum duration of time. Dr. Craig rejects this idea in his thesis, but I think it has merit. Let me explain. A hypothetical minimum amount of time is often called a "chronon." Time may be infinitely divisible in thought, but in reality can only be broken down to a minimum duration, like an atom of time. (Not a perfect example. We can obviously divide atoms into more elementary particles, but you get the point.) Then we could say that the present "chronon" is what composes the present. This would cause time to unfold like a movie, with successive pictures that blend together so quickly that it blends seamlessly into a continuous picture. Craig rejects this because of Zeno's Stadium Paradox.[12] It goes like this:

Suppose there are three rows of atoms, and three in each row. So it looks like this:

Row 1	1	2	3
Row 2	1	2	3
Row 3	1	2	3

Now suppose row 1 is moving to the left at a rate of one space per chronon, row 3 is moving to the right at a rate of one space per chronon, and row 2 is sitting still. At chronon 1, we have the picture above. That means at chronon 2, the picture will look like this:

Row 1	1	2	3		
Row 2		1	2	3	
Row 3			1	2	3

What this means is there was never a time when the 2 in row 1 was aligned with the 1 in row 3. But they obviously passed each other. It would seem to imply that if time is made of chronons, reality jumped from one state to another. However, I think we can solve this with an analogy from distance.

---

12   Dr. William Craig, *Time and Eternity*, 158

According to the uncertainty principle in quantum physics, there is a smallest measurable length called the "Plank length." It's 10^{-20} times smaller than the diameter of a proton. If we could see it, we would literally see the "fabric" of space. At any distance smaller than this, the concept of distance and space breaks down and becomes meaningless. In other words, nothing can travel a shorter distance than a Plank length. So we may ask the same question as Zeno's paradox of motion. In order to move one Plank length, I would first have to cross half of it, but I can't because the Plank length is the shortest distance there is. So I, along with Zeno, would have to conclude that motion is impossible. But it obviously isn't. I think Zeno's stadium paradox is similar to his paradox of motion. Our everyday experience disproves it.

But say you don't buy that. Then we can return to Craig's solution, namely that time is conceptually prior to any mathematization of it. The question "How long is the present" is not a question about reality. We can ask how long the present minute is, and the answer is one minute, and that's fine. There is no minimum duration. Time is composed of an indefinite number of instants, which we may divide into chronons if we like. The present moment is however long you want to measure it.

McTaggart's Paradox

John McTaggart is the black sheep of the philosophy of time. He doesn't hold to A-theory or B-theory. In 1908, he published his article, "The Unreality of Time." The man successfully reasoned himself into a corner, and was forced to conclude that time did not exist. Basically he showed that A-theory must be right, and then he showed that A-theory can't be right. We've already looked through the reasons why A-theory is right, so there is no need to re-hash that part of the argument here. So let's move on to the second part.

McTaggart defined temporal becoming as an event transitioning from the future to the present, and then to the past. As time marches forward, it passes events one by one, changing their tense as it does so. Therefore every event changes tense. It is in the future, then for a moment it is in the present, then it is in the past. This is the only change that events go through. Beyond that, they simply exist.

Here's the problem. Pastness, presentness, and futureness aren't compatible with each other. They are mutually exclusive. So how can any event possibly have all three? Every event exists on the timeline, and therefore has presentness, pastness, and futureness. You could say that the event no longer has futureness when it becomes present, but why should the present be privileged in such a way? If there is a guy located at the event in the future, to him, that event is present. Every event is past, present, and future, which it obviously can't be. Maybe you could say that a certain time doesn't just have presentness at a certain time, but just has presentness, period. When that certain time is absolutely present, then it is not also past and future, so there is no contradiction. But this is to postulate a sort of "hyper-time," and then you run into the same paradox in said hyper-time. (I know this is getting weird. The point is just how inescapable the problem is, as presented.)

So how do we solve this? The problem is in McTaggart's conception of what an event becoming "present" means. When we refer to an event becoming present, on A-theory, we literally mean that it becomes "real." Before that, it did not exist, not even in the future. It didn't have a future tense because it did not exist at all. This is called "presentism": the idea that the only reality that exists is the present one. The past is literally gone forever and the future literally does not exist yet. Temporal becoming is not an event exchanging future tense for present tense. Rather, temporal becoming is something coming into existence. The only properties possessed by anything are what it currently possesses in the present. The only tense an event ever has is present tense.

Presentism is sometimes rejected because, if combined with STR, it would imply that you alone exist. But we've already seen that STR doesn't disprove universal time, so that isn't a problem. Another objection to presentism is that if it were true, we couldn't make any comparisons between the present and the past, because the past does not exist. But why do two members of a comparison have to exist at the same time? Also, if this were true, then we couldn't make hypothetical comparisons either. I couldn't say for example, that if I had finished that burrito from earlier, I would be one pound heavier than I am right now, and possibly experiencing some regret for past actions.

What McTaggart proved is that any attempt to merge the A and B theories of time will fail miserably. But if we take A-theory seriously, there is no future, and therefore there is no paradox.

This Had Better Be Going Somewhere

So where does that leave us? God exists and time is not an illusion. I'm still suffering in this evil, terrible, indifferent world of real time that God made. God created three dimensions of space and one dimension of time, filled it with matter and energy, and called it good. He lied! It is far from good.

Hang on, dear reader. We are getting closer. We now know that time passes for us here in the universe. But does it pass for the maker of the universe? Nothing we've seen so far would show that God, the maker of time, is bound to it in some way. But what if he were?

CHAPTER 10

TIME FOR CHANGE

The ancient Greek philosophers, and indeed many since them, would consider the idea of God in time ridiculous. God is the most perfect being. Time implies change, and to change was considered to be imperfect. Also, perfection was thought to imply simplicity, and to change is to introduce complexity. But the ancient Greeks didn't know that the universe had a beginning, and that changes everything.

The Big Change

About fourteen billion years ago, there was nothing. Nothing existed. Not matter. Not space. Not time. *Then,* the universe! Something *changed.* There was nothing, *then* there was something. God created the universe, with dimensions of space and time and temporal becoming is real. What this means is that God existed without the universe, *then* God existed with the universe. At the first moment of time, God experienced change. And without time, there is no change. By the very act of creation, God is now temporal.

Defenders of divine timelessness often assert that to place God in time is to take away his omniscience, because even a perfect memory and foreknowledge is not as good as being present at every moment. But we can turn the tables at this point. To place God outside of time is to severely limit his knowledge. What is happening in the universe is constantly changing. If God knows everything, then he knows what is happening in the universe. Therefore, God's knowledge is constantly changing. He knows what events are taking place "now," and that knowledge is in constant flux. He knows what is "present." If God is timeless, he cannot know what is "now." He has no understanding of tense. Nothing about his knowledge, or any characteristic about him, can ever change. Also, if God is timeless, he is no longer omnipotent, because he is no longer free to interact with the world. He cannot sustain or cause any events, because events occur in time. Traditionally this logic has been denied by appealing to Minkowski spacetime, but we've seen that this doesn't work. For God to be omniscient or omnipotent, God must be temporal.

Now you, humble reader, may think that I have just reasoned myself into a corner. You may be recalling Hilbert and Tristram, and realizing that I just made God impossible. If God is in time, and God did not begin to exist, then we face all the same problems of infinite regress that we faced with the universe itself. And if God did begin to exist, then we must find a cause for God. And you are correct. But why couldn't the very first change that occurs in God be a change from timelessness to temporality? Before the creation of the universe, God could exist in a timeless, changeless, perfect state of being. Then, at the moment of the big bang, God becomes temporal. God becomes related to his creation.

McTaggart Strikes Again

God looked down from heaven upon the children of men, to see if there were any that did understand, that did seek God. – Psalm 53:2

I can't recall the exact moment when it clicked. I was at work. I was lost in my head, thinking about all the competing ideas I had read. Ideas on time, on God's knowledge, on the problem of evil. How utterly inadequate the answers given seemed to be. My mind went to McTaggart, and then suddenly out of nowhere, something clicked. All the pieces of the puzzle spinning around in my head fit together in a beautiful picture. And I had a sneaking suspicion that I had just thought myself into a whole new view of life. I needed to write it down. I needed to flesh it out. I needed to look at all the implications. In my hotel that night, I was pacing. I couldn't sleep. What I'm about to propose has not, to my knowledge, been proposed before. This is the linchpin of my apologetic.

McTaggart showed that time is real. We have seen that to be the case. He also showed that things cannot be past, present, and future, and we have seen that he was right. This leaves us with presentism: that only the present is real. The past is gone forever and the future is yet to come. If someone were to ask me to define the past, a proper definition would be "what has happened." The past is composed of all the events that have occurred. It would seem then, that a proper definition of the future is: "what will happen." The future is composed of all the events that will occur. God is essentially omniscient. He knows the past, present, and future. He knows everything that has happened, everything that is happening, and everything that will happen.

But I submit to you, dear reader, along with McTaggart, that this is not the case. The future is not what *will* happen. The future is what *has not* happened. And that difference is crucial. There are no future events. The future is not real. *The future is exactly the same as nothing.*

God, being an omniscient being, knows everything. *And he doesn't know the future.* God knows every single thing there is to know. There is nothing to know in the future. The future is nothing. And if you say that God must know the future because God is omniscient, McTaggart is right there to show you otherwise. If future events exist in the mind of God, then future events exist, and McTaggart's paradox returns to make time unreal. But time is very real, and so is God. You might say that this reasoning makes it impossible for God to remember the past, but I don't think that is the case. Past events are not real, but we can remember them because they were real at one time. There was a time when those events were present. We can remember them because they had "realness." But the future has never been real. Remember, temporal becoming is a reality. Memory and foreknowledge are vastly different things. The future is nothing, and to foreknow it is the same as to know nothing.

When it hit me, the very foundations of what I thought I believed came crashing down. The walls tumbled, revealing the light. The implications began to mount at an overwhelming pace. To borrow a phrase from the Bible, the old things had passed away and everything was new.

For the Sake of Love

Imagine with me for a moment, the dawn of time. Logically prior to the big bang, God exists perfectly. Timelessly. Completely self-contained and self-satisfied. He is all powerful. Nothing can limit him. But power is not his essence. It is something he has, no doubt. He has all the power there is. But essence is the properties that a thing contains which, were it to lose them, it would cease to be. A thing can have any number of properties that aren't part of its essence. What if God's essence is love? What if the creator of the universe wanted a creation that would freely choose to be a part of his essence? A creation that would choose to love him. What if, for the sake of love, God made time?

CHAPTER 11

EUTHYPHRO'S FALSE DILEMMA

God is real. Time is real. God is in time. God is omniscient. There is no future. God does not know it. I am truly free, in the most libertarian sense. None of my actions are determined. I am entirely responsible for every good and bad deed I do. It is now possible that God is good. However, I have not shown this. Not yet. All I've shown is that God is not necessarily evil. We now have one last step to take before we crest the hill, and the grand picture is revealed. The final question: "Is God good?"

Euthyphro and South Park

I have a confession. I love the TV show South Park. Buried beneath all the poop jokes and general foulness is some really intelligent and original writing. Anyway, there's a really old episode where Stan's grandpa turns 102 years old and wants to die. He keeps trying to get the kids to kill him. He adds "kill Grandpa" to Stan's list of chores and trash talks Cartman's mom to make Cartman mad. Stan keeps going around town asking people if it's "ok to kill someone if they want you to." Mr. Garrison says, "I'm not touching that with a twenty foot pole." Chef says, "I'm not touching that with a forty foot pole." Kyle suggests to Stan that "maybe you should ask the Lord for guidance." In the show, Jesus runs a daytime talk show called "Jesus and Pals." So Stan calls in to Jesus and Pals.

"Jesus?"

"Yes, my son?"

"Jesus, is it okay to kill somebody if they ask you to, because they're in a lot of pain? You know, like assisted suicide is that okay?"

"My son?"

"Yes?"

"I'm not touching that with a sixty foot pole."

It's a quality joke. And it draws from Euthyphro's dilemma. Plato proposed the question: Is it good because the gods will it, or do the gods will it because it is good?

The Moral Argument

This is a common argument used to show the existence of God just like the cosmological and teleological arguments. I omitted it before, because it fits in better at this stage of the journey. A common form of the moral argument can be arranged in a modus ponens, and it goes like this.

1. If God does not exist, objective moral values and duties do not exist.
2. Objective moral values and duties do exist.
3. Therefore, God exists.

Before we go any further, we need to distinguish between what is right and what is good, because they aren't the same.

When referring to moral values, we are talking about what is good. You are not obligated by moral values. It is a good thing for you to give money to charity. It is also a good thing to save money to set aside for your child's college education. But you are not obligated to do both. It is a good thing for you to be a doctor, and it is a good thing for you to be a philosopher, but both are full-time jobs, so you have to pick. Moral duties, on the other hand, are obligatory. We are obligated to abstain from things like murder, rape, and theft, and we are compelled to behave justly and kindly. Second, it is important to emphasize that the moral argument is about *objective* moral values and duties. Objective means independent of what you or I or anyone thinks. It is saying that things are good or bad or right or wrong independent of anyone's opinion on the matter. It is saying that, even if the entire world agreed that murder was fine, it would still be wrong. It is saying that slavery was wrong even when most people in the United States didn't see a problem with it.

So let's talk about morality. In theism, humans hold a special distinction from other life. We are rational, free creatures, made in God's image. (When we say "made in God's image" we mean that God is also rational and free.) We are "like" God in this sense. And we have seen that this freedom is not an illusion. Now, while the moral argument is a powerful argument for the existence of God, it is not necessary for me to unpack all the points here. We are way past the question, "Does God exist?" Any additional evidence to that is just extra icing on a well iced cake at this point.

It is worth noting though, that moral relativism is mostly a thing of the past. And without God, moral relativism is exactly what we are left with. Animals rape, murder, and eat one another all the time. It is a very natural thing. If we hold no special distinction from other animals, then the most a rapist can be accused of is acting unsociably. Again, we are talking about objective moral duties here. No one is saying that an atheist can't live an upstanding moral life. No one is saying that there are no Christian or Jewish or Muslim hypocrites. Indeed I count myself among them. No one is saying that we can't craft a valid code of ethics without reference to God. There are vast numbers of people that don't believe in God and do believe in objective right and wrong, and live their lives accordingly.

What I'm saying is that, without God, there is no objective basis for right and wrong. Put another way, God has to exist for morality to exist, but you don't have to believe in God for morality to exist, or to live morally. But this leaves us with a dilemma, as proposed by Plato. Is it good because God wills it, or does God will it because it is good? If it's good because God wills it, then good becomes arbitrary. God could have willed genocide to be good, and we would be obligated to commit genocide. But if God wills it because it's good, then moral value and duty becomes independent of God, and no explanatory progress of moral objectivity has been made.

Fortunately, the Euthyphro dilemma is a false one, and serves to put one of the last pieces of this puzzle in place. It isn't good because God wills it. God doesn't will it because it is good.

God wills it because God is good.

Moral value and duty is a reflection of God's essence. Again, an essence is what makes something what it is. It is an attribute that something has by necessity, and if it loses that attribute, it ceases to be. If a tree lost "matter" it would not be a tree. If I lost "mammal," I would not be human. "Good" is part of God's essence. We, in his image, comprehend morality. While we certainly disagree on it in many respects, we all know that it exists, and that we should live by it. Indeed, it motivates the central "bad question" of this book. "How can I believe in a God who …" Regardless of how that blank is filled in, we are asking how we could believe in a God who would allow some sort of pain and suffering. The second question, "Is God evil?" is meaningless if there is no objective morality.

Now at this point, it is still possible that God is evil. We could, with equal logical validity, say that there is objective good and evil not because God's essence is good, but because God's essence is evil. In other words, we could ask the opposite question of Plato. "Is it evil because God wills it, or does God will it because it is evil?"

To answer this objection, I can take one of two routes. One is the ontological argument for God's necessary existence as the greatest conceivable being. While this argument is championed by several prominent philosophers, most notably Alvin Plantinga, I have reservations about it, and so I will not be taking that route here. (I'll refer you to him for the ontological argument, and you can decide for yourself.) I must instead take a turn toward theology and historical biblical criticism. I must turn to the reliability of the accounts of the life, death, and resurrection of Jesus of Nazareth, and there is enough to say about that to fill a whole separate book. In fact, this task has already been taken care of by many people before me.

If you are not a Christian, dear reader, then you may abandon this book now. It is time for you to assess for yourself the accuracy and reliability of the gospels. N.T. Wright and once again William Craig are good places to start. I think you will find, as I did, that the gospels are historically accurate to a very high degree. They probably aren't inerrant, but they're about as reliable as an historical document can be. I think you will find, as I did, that the disciples were neither deceivers nor deceived, and that Jesus was God incarnate. That he really took your sin upon himself, and really rose from the dead. Love died, and then conquered death.

I wish you luck in your study and search for truth. When you're finished, come back and finish this book.

For those of you that already call yourselves Christians, read on! This is where everything comes together. This is where we find hope. This is where we find love. This is where the dark glass is removed and we see our maker face to face.

CHAPTER 12

ME VS. THE PROPHETS

Hello brother or sister in Christ. Thanks for sticking with me this far. You probably have a lot of questions, concerns, and maybe even strong objections to what I've just proposed, and I understand. It's different to put it lightly. Let me calm one major concern right from the start. Like I said before, I am not in any way saying that God is not omniscient. He most definitely is. I am not challenging that. What I'm challenging is the nature of time, and the nature of what exists to be known.

Another major concern for you is probably how this hypothesis integrates with scripture. This is a valid and important concern, and I will admit something to you right now. It doesn't fit perfectly. If you accept what I've presented, you will be forced to abandon the doctrine of biblical inerrancy. But before you stop reading, let me make a couple of points. First, just because you abandon the doctrine of biblical inerrancy, that doesn't force you to abandon the doctrine of biblical *inspiration*. I still firmly believe that the Bible is the inspired word of God. I just think that its human authors made an error or two, which we humans tend to do at times. Second, though it doesn't line up perfectly, I think you'll be surprised to find that my hypothesis lines up *really well*.

In fact, in my humble opinion, it lines up better than the classical view of divine omniscience.

In the coming pages, I'll look at some of the best examples of support, as well as a lot of the passages typically used to show God's exhaustive knowledge of the future. I think you'll be convinced that they don't show that at all. Fortunately for me, a lot of the biblical scholarship has already been done for me. There is a relatively new line of thought called "Open Theism" that is very similar to what I have presented here. Open Theism holds that God faces a *partially* open and *partially* settled future. In other words, God determines what he chooses to determine and leaves open what he chooses to leave open. It posits that scripture has two motifs when describing the future. There are passages that demonstrate God's certainty about what will happen, and there are passages that demonstrate a God who risks, reacts to events, and changes his mind. Traditionally, only the first motif has been taken as literal, while the second has been taken as anthropomorphic descriptions of God. Open theists argue that both should be taken literally. So open theists start with the Bible, and build a worldview from there. The biggest difference here is that up until this point, the Bible has barely entered the discussion. I mostly philosophized my way to this point. So I think it's worth something that I wound up with such a similar conclusion.

I'm arguing instead that, due to McTaggart's paradox and God's relationship to time, he must face an *entirely* open future. Granted, his complete knowledge of all things present and his perfect memory of all things past would let him predict most things to a high degree of certainty. But *everything* about the future is still a probability. Even to God. So let's dig into Scripture and see what we find. I'll start with some of the passages that seem to be most strongly against my hypothesis.

God: "I don't change."

"I the Lord do not change." Malachi 3:6. Seems about as straightforward as it gets. And in Isaiah we get passages like "I am God, and there is no one like me, declaring the end from the beginning and from ancient times things not yet done." God is pretty much saying "I know the future," right? It's even more explicit two chapters later. "The former things I declared long ago, they went out from my mouth and I made them known; then suddenly I did them and they came to pass." How can it get more obvious? A well-known open theist named Gregory Boyd breaks up the scriptural motif of God's future knowledge into five categories.

1. Foreknowledge of his chosen people. Examples:
   a. In Genesis 15 he tells Abraham how his offspring would be slaves in Egypt for four hundred years but would come out with great possessions.
   b. In Jeremiah 29 he tells Israel that he will fulfill his promise to bring them back to Jerusalem.

2. Foreknowledge of individuals
   a. In 1st Kings, God predicts that Josiah will tear down the pagan altars and destroy the pagan priesthood in Israel before Josiah is ever born.
   b. In the gospels, Jesus predicts that Peter will deny him three times, that Peter would die as a martyr, and that Judas would betray him just to name a few.
   c. David says in Psalm 139 that, "In your book were written all the days that were formed for me when none of them yet existed."
   d. God appointed Jeremiah to be a "prophet to the nations" in the first chapter of Jeremiah and set Paul

apart in the first chapter of Galatians, both said to have happened before they were born.

    e.   Daniel is full of pretty specific prophesy, like the succession of the four kingdoms, and God predicts the fall of Tyre in Ezekiel. All of this information involved actions of Alexander the Great, centuries before that guy was born.

3.   Foreknowledge of Christ's ministry. Examples:

    a.   One of the most blatant examples is 1 Peter 1:19-20 - "But with the precious blood of Christ, as of a lamb without blemish and without spot. Who verily was foreordained before the foundation of the world, but was manifest in these last times for you."

    b.   In Zachariah 12, God tells Israel that they will "look upon the one whom they have pierced" and "mourn for him."

    c.   Isaiah 53 is full of specific predictions about the crucifixion.

    d.   Jesus himself predicted many things about his own death, such as that he would "suffer at the hands of the elders and chief priests and scribes, and would be raised on the third day," (Matthew 16). Acts 2 confirms that this was according to the plan and foreknowledge of God.

4.   Foreknowledge of the elect. Examples:

    a.   Paul, in the main verse used in favor of predestination says "those whom he foreknew, he also predestined to be conformed to the image of his Son." (Romans 8:29). Then he says in Ephesians 1 that "He chose us in Christ before the foundation of the world to be holy and blameless before him in love."

b. In 2nd Timothy, we are told that we were chosen and given grace before the world began, which would seem unnecessary if we didn't yet need grace because we hadn't yet sinned.

5. Foreknowledge of the end of time.
   a. Paul says in 1st Timothy that "in the later times some will renounce the faith by paying attention to deceitful spirits and teachings of demons," who "forbid marriage and demand abstinence from foods."
   b. The book of Revelation is pretty much entirely read as a prediction of the end of time.

Obviously, I didn't cover every verse in the Bible pertaining to this issue. That would take at least a whole other book. It would probably take several books. Still, I hit most of the highlights, and I encourage you to dig deeper after you're done reading this. Now, let's go back through these categories one by one and re-examine them. It may be a bit tedious. Biblical exegesis can be that way. But if my entire philosophy is at odds with the majority of the Bible, that would be a serious mark against it, so I'd say it's worth the effort. So let's do this.

Round Two

Before I even get to the categories listed above, let's address those verses in Isaiah I used to introduce this whole thing. A quick re-examination will reveal that they aren't nearly as conclusive as we might have thought. In Isaiah 46, immediately after God says, "I am God, and there is no one like me, declaring the end from the beginning and from ancient times things not yet done," he adds, "My purpose shall stand, and I will fulfill my intention. I have spoken, and I will bring it to pass. I have planned, and I will do it." So it seems that God is not talking about foreknowledge at all, but rather his own intention to bring something to pass. Indeed this passage seems to make more sense if God *doesn't* know the future. He is assuring Israel that, regardless of any evil or obstacles the future may hold, he is all powerful, and he will fulfill his good intentions. The same applies to Isaiah 48. God said, "The former things I declared long ago, they went out from my mouth and I made them known; then suddenly *I did them* and they came to pass." God is saying that he won't go back on his promises. If he says he'll do something, you can trust him to do it. It's in this sense that he "doesn't change." Now let's look at the five categories again.

1. Foreknowledge of his chosen people.

   In Genesis God let Israel remain in captivity for four hundred years, and then again in Jeremiah for seventy years (referring to the Babylonian captivity.) I don't see any reason that God would need to know the future to make this happen. He could use any number of free agents and circumstances to bring this about. These are very broad prophesies about large groups of people. Any natural scientist can tell you it is a lot easier to predict the behavior of an ant colony than the behavior of one ant. I think that same principle applies here.

2. Foreknowledge of individuals

   The prophesy about Josiah is difficult to reconcile, I admit. The prophesy is hundreds of years before his birth. But why is it necessary that, at the time of the prophesy, Josiah be a specific man? God could still use anyone to fulfill the purpose he had. And at the proper time, he found two parents situated in the right circumstances who, based on God's complete knowledge of their past actions, character, and innermost thoughts, he used to bring Josiah into the world. He knew how they would raise their child, and he knew he could orchestrate the circumstances to make him king, and redeem Israel. Again, this is speculation, but I don't see why it isn't possible.

What about Peter's denial? Jesus predicted it in a very specific way. But it seems this can be explained similarly to the prophecy about Josiah. God knows us better than we know ourselves. Jesus knew Peter's character. Jesus knew that Peter thought the messiah would be a military leader, leading the Jewish people to victory over their enemies. He knew that, once Peter realized this wasn't the case, his confidence in the Messiah would be severely shaken. All that was left was to create a situation where Peter would be asked about his association with Jesus when he was most vulnerable.

How about Judas's betrayal? When the Bible says that Jesus knew "from the first" that Judas would betray him, but the same phrase can be interpreted as "early on." So it could simply mean that Judas decided "early on" to betray Jesus, and then of course, being omniscient, Jesus knew this. Judas fulfilled prophesy. But there is no reason why it had to be him. Judas chose to be a "son of perdition." He is not a pawn in God's grand game. He is a main character in a gut wrenching tragedy. Life and death were set before him, as with all men. He chose death. He betrayed his savior. In fact, I see no reason why everyone who had a hand in the death of the savior can't be viewed in this way. They were lost souls, who managed to play a part in the redeeming of the world.

A similar point can be made regarding scripture about God's plans for people's lives. God set Paul and Jeremiah apart for a special purpose. He had a plan for their lives, and they followed it. But again, they could have been tragic characters.

They could have chosen not to follow God's plan. Paul says as much to King Agrippa in Acts 26.

What about Psalm 139? How does God number our days in his book if he doesn't know how many there will be? As a first point, the Psalms are poetry, and literal translations of them are rarely appropriate. But even if we do take a literal translation, the KJV Bible translates what was planned not as "days" but as "members." It says "Thine eyes did see my substance yet being unperfect; and in thy book all my members were written." In the verses before, the psalmist is talking about God forming him in his mother's womb. So it is very likely this verse is not talking about God writing down his days in a ledger, but about God crafting his body before his birth.

As far as the rise and fall of nations prophesied in Daniel, again, large groups of people are far more predictable than individuals. Alexander the Great was used to fulfill prophecy. But if not for him, there could have been any number of other ways to fulfill God's plans.

3. Foreknowledge of Christ's ministry

1st Peter says that the incarnation and crucifixion were part of God's plan "before the foundation of the world." At first, I thought that this verse simply didn't fit. At the beginning of time, God would have no idea whether his creation would accept or reject him. The entire point of creating us was for us to choose to love him. At first, I thought, this verse posed a serious problem. But now, I think it makes perfect sense. God made us with free will. So obviously, he knew we could choose to reject him. Being good and loving in essence, he couldn't bear the thought of condemning us forever, so he made a contingency plan. For the unthinkable. For the possibility that we would reject life and choose death, as we did. And all the specific details about the crucifixion never include the person who will do them. Any free agent would do. Any tragic character who was offered light but sought the darkness.

4. Foreknowledge of the Elect

When Paul says that we were predestined, he isn't talking about individuals. He's talking about everyone. He says as much in 1st Timothy 2: "For this is good and acceptable in the sight of God our Savior. Who will have all men to be saved, and to come unto the knowledge of the truth." God's will is that all "be holy and blameless before him in love." God wants us to choose to share his essence. Indeed, Romans 8, the most common verse used in support of classical divine foreknowledge, undermines the view its proponents claim that it supports. It says "Those whom he foreknew, he predestined." This would imply that he didn't foreknow everything. I would say that God predestined all who choose him to grow closer to him and his Son. Preferably, that would be everyone.

5. Prophecies about the End Times

Paul, and all the New Testament authors, believed that they were living in the last days. This is an important fact to remember when reading them. Most of what they refer to in the "last days" is referring to their own imminent future. Regarding Revelation, it is an important point that interpreting this book as being about the end of time is a very recent phenomenon. In Biblical exegesis, a fundamental rule is to read the text as it would have been read by its original intended audience. For example, for a first century Christian, "the beast" is probably Nero. There are tons of interpretations of the book of Revelation, and I am far from an expert on the subject. But the important point for us here is that there *are* a lot of interpretations.

Again, there is plenty more scripture to analyze. I encourage you to do so. But even from these highlights I think you can see that it is possible to call yourself a Bible believing follower of God and hold to the hypothesis presented in this book. And it gets even better. So far, all we've looked at is all the scripture that seems to discredit my hypothesis. We've seen that it mostly does not. We haven't even started to look at all the Biblical support that my hypothesis enjoys. And there's plenty of it.

CHAPTER 13

ME VS. THE PROPHETS 2: WE MADE UP

The picture of God as a being who doesn't know the future is strong in the Bible. Very strong. Much stronger than you might realize. The scripture consistently and explicitly depicts God as a personal being who reacts, feels, and is affected by changing situations. I must make an important point before I delve into Scripture again. The only thing necessary for my hypothesis to be correct is for God to interact, on any level, with creation. If God is in time, I argue, the future is not real and is therefore unknowable. Scripture is, at its core, the story of redemption. It mostly consists of God interacting with creation. Restoring it. Making it right again. So any verses that suggest that God doesn't know the future simply add to the strength of the hypothesis. Again, the open theist Gregory Boyd has categorized this motif nicely, and I'll be presenting a summary of his work in this chapter. Let's look at some examples.

God Regrets

- Genesis 6:6: "And it repented the Lord that he had made man on the earth, and it grieved him at his heart."
- 1ˢᵗ Samuel 13:13: "And Samuel said to Saul, Thou hast done foolishly: thou hast not kept the commandment of the Lord thy God, which he commanded thee: for now would the Lord have established thy kingdom upon Israel forever."
- 1ˢᵗ Samuel 15:35: "And Samuel came no more to see Saul until the day of his death: nevertheless Samuel mourned for Saul: and the Lord repented that he had made Saul king over Israel."

These are just a few examples of God explicitly and directly stating that he feels regret about things *that he did.* What reason would he have to feel regret if he not only knew but caused every event? What's more, if God is timeless, he could not feel anything, because to experience a feeling requires a change. God was genuinely saddened by the wickedness of man before the flood. He genuinely repented of it. He established Saul as the king of Israel, because he was a godly man. But then Saul rebelled. He was a free agent, and he turned his back on God. And God repented that he had made Saul king.

God Confronts the Unexpected

- Isaiah 5:2,4: "And he fenced it, and gathered out the stones thereof, and planted it with the choicest vine, and built a tower in the midst of it, and also made a winepress therein: and he looked that it should bring forth grapes, and it brought forth wild grapes.... What could have been done more to my vineyard, that I have not done in it? Wherefore, when I looked that it should bring forth grapes, brought it forth wild grapes?"

- Jeremiah 3:19-20: "But I said, How shall I put thee among the children, and give thee a pleasant land, a goodly heritage of the hosts of nations? And I said, Thou shalt call me, My father; and shalt not turn away from me. Surely as a wife treacherously departeth from her husband, so have ye dealt treacherously with me, O house of Israel, saith the Lord."
- Jeremiah 19:5: "They have built also the high places of Baal, to burn their sons with fire for burnt offerings unto Baal, which I commanded not, nor spake it, neither came it into my mind."

If God knows the future, how can he say that the Israelites offering sacrifices to Baal never entered his mind? It was obviously in his mind for all eternity. This is a clear contradiction. What reason is there not to take God at his word on this one? He couldn't believe his chosen people, for whom he had done so much, would turn to an idol. It never entered his mind. He expected Israel to bring forth grapes, but they acted contrary to his expectation. It is stated plainly.

God Gets Frustrated

- Exodus 4:12-15: "Now therefore go, and I will be with thy mouth, and teach thee what thou shalt say. And he said, 'O my Lord, send, I pray thee, by the hand of him whom thou wilt send.' And the anger of the Lord was kindled against Moses, and he said, 'Is not Aaron the Levite thy brother? I know that he can speak well. And also, behold, he cometh forth to meet thee: and when he seeth thee, he will be glad in his heart.'"

- Ezekiel 22: 30-31: "And I sought for a man among them, that should make up the hedge, and stand in the gap before me for the land, that I should not destroy it: but I found none. Therefore have I poured out mine indignation upon them; I have consumed them with the fire of my wrath: their own way have I recompensed upon their heads, saith the Lord God."

- Tons of examples of God's plans of judgment being reversed or delayed. (Exodus 32, Numbers 11, 14, 16, Deuteronomy 9, Judges 10, 2nd Samuel 24, 1st Kings 21, 2nd Kings 13, 20, 2nd Chronicles 12.)

Even putting aside for a moment that all of these verses depict God interacting in time with his creation, it is difficult to see how or why God would seek for someone to pray to him in Ezekiel when he knew there would be no one. It is hard to understand why he would express frustration at Moses's timidity if he knew everything he would say and do in advance.

God Tests People

- Genesis 22:12: "And he said, Lay not thine hand upon the lad, neither do thou any thing unto him: for now I know that thou fearest God, seeing thou hast not withheld thy son, thine only son from me."

- Deuteronomy 8:2: "And thou shalt remember all the way which the Lord thy God led thee these forty years in the wilderness, to humble thee, and to prove thee, to know what was in thine heart, whether thou wouldest keep his commandments, or no."

- Deuteronomy 13:1-3: "If there arise among you a prophet, or a dreamer of dreams, and giveth thee a sign or a wonder. And the sign or the wonder come to pass, whereof he spake unto thee, saying, Let us go after other gods, which thou hast not known, and let us serve them; Thou shalt not hearken unto the words of that prophet, or that dreamer of dreams: for the Lord your God proveth you, to know whether ye love the Lord your God with all your heart and with all your soul."
- Exodus 16:4: "Then said the Lord unto Moses, Behold, I will rain bread from heaven for you; and the people shall go out and gather a certain rate every day, that I may prove them, whether they will walk in my law, or no."

Traditionally, when confronted with verses such as these, defenders of the traditional view of God will say that such testing was so that those tested would discover something about themselves, not so God would discover anything. But that isn't what the verses say at all. In fact, I don't see how God could state it any clearer than he does. When Abraham nearly kills his only son, God says "for now *I know* that thou fearest God." He doesn't say "for now *you* know." God is testing the character of Abraham, to find out *for himself.* The same holds for all the other examples.

God Talks About What May Happen

To start this one, let's go back to Exodus 4, when God gets frustrated with Moses. This is the result of a long bargaining session God and Moses are having. God assigns Moses to the task of freeing the Israelites in Chapter 3. He assures Moses that the elders will listen to him, but Moses has doubts. He opens Chapter 4 by telling God "But, behold, they will not believe me, nor hearken unto my voice: for they will say, The Lord hath not appeared unto thee." God responds by turning Moses's staff into a snake "That they *may* believe that the Lord God of their fathers, the God of Abraham, the God of Isaac, and the God of Jacob, hath appeared unto thee." (emphasis added.) Moses is still doubtful, so God makes Moses's hand leprous, then normal again, then says, "And it shall come to pass, *if they will not believe thee,* neither hearken to the voice of the first sign, that they will believe the voice of the latter sign." (emphasis added.) God goes on, "And it shall come to pass, if they will not believe also these two signs, neither hearken unto thy voice, that thou shalt take of the water of the river, and pour it upon the dry land: and the water which thou takest out of the river shall become blood upon the dry land."

That's a lot of "ifs" for a being that knows the future. If the traditional view of God is true, he knew not only how long it would take to convince Moses, but also how many miracles it would take get the elders to believe Moses, and would have known and been the cause of both things from the dawn of time. This verse is a clear depiction of God working with libertarian freedom of individuals to achieve his goals.

There are other examples too. God says in Exodus 13 that he didn't lead Israel on the shortest route to the promised land "Lest peradventure the people repent when they see war, and they return to Egypt." God was concerned about the *possibility* of the Israelites witnessing war and returning to Egypt and captivity. Another good example is God's command to Jeremiah to preach so that, "If so be they will hearken, and turn every man from his evil way, that I may repent me of the evil, which I purpose to do unto them because of the evil of their doings." If Israel's fate was certain, why would God deceive them into thinking they could change it? But it makes total sense if their fate was not determined. God is pleading with them to return to him. To love him. To be his chosen.

Perhaps the most moving example comes from Jesus himself, in the garden of Gethsemane, as he faces his death. He knows his time has come. He is about to fulfill his contingency plan for us. We did the unthinkable, and God hasn't abandoned us. But Jesus knows what he is about to face and, being fully man, feels fear. More fear than I could possibly imagine. He says to his heavenly father, "O my Father, if it be possible, let this cup pass from me: nevertheless not as I will, but as thou wilt." Jesus knew what he had to do, but his fear made him desperately search for any other option. Any possibility of avoiding the agonizing physical, mental, and spiritual pain of crucifixion and bearing the sin of all mankind.

God Talks About His Return

- 2nd Peter 3:9: "The Lord is not slack concerning his promise, as some men count slackness; but is longsuffering to us, not willing that any should perish, but that all should come to repentance."
- Mark 13:32: "But of that day and that hour knoweth no man, no, not the angels which are in heaven, neither the Son, but the Father."
- Revelation 3:5: "He that overcometh, the same shall be clothed in white raiment; and I will not blot out his name out of the book of life, but I will confess his name before my Father, and before his angels."

God has delayed his return so that more people might repent and come back to his saving grace and redemption. If the future is set, the delay is a contradiction. You might be wondering how to reconcile this with Mark 13, which says that the Father knows the date of the Son's return. First it should be mentioned that according to the doctrine of the Trinity, there is nothing one member knows that another does not. We Christians don't worship three gods. We worship one God composed of three parts. (Interestingly enough, the doctrine of the Trinity stands in stark opposition to the doctrine of divine simplicity, which is often used as an argument for God's timelessness.) That's why I think it makes more sense to interpret this verse as it lying within the *authority* of the Father to determine the date of his Son's return. It's his decision. But that doesn't mean he's decided yet.

As for the "Book of Life", what reason would God have to "blot out" a name if the fate of said name was determined? Why bother writing it in the wrong book? Even under compatibilist theories like Molinism, that doesn't make sense.

Reversed Intentions

- 1ˢᵗ Chronicles 21:15: "And God sent an angel unto Jerusalem to destroy it: and as he was destroying, the Lord beheld, and he repented him of the evil, and said to the angel that destroyed, 'It is enough, stay now thine hand.' And the angel of the Lord stood by the threshing floor of Ornan the Jebusite."
- Jeremiah 26:19: "Did Hezekiah king of Judah and all Judah put him at all to death? Did he not fear the Lord, and besought the Lord, and the Lord repented him of the evil which he had pronounced against them? Thus might we procure great evil against our souls."
- Exodus 32:14: "And the Lord repented of the evil which he thought to do unto his people."

This list could go on for another twenty pages, seriously. Examples of God changing his mind based on human repentance or prayer on behalf of another permeate the scripture. God cares about our actions. He cares about our prayers. He reacts to them. He *changes* his mind.

Jeremiah and the Potter

One of the passages often used to demonstrate God's exhaustive knowledge and control of the future is, ironically, one of the passages that I believe shows just the opposite. It's Jeremiah 18:1-10.

> *"The word which came to Jeremiah from the Lord, saying, 'Arise, and go down to the potter's house, and there I will cause thee to hear my words.' Then I went down to the potter's house, and, behold, he wrought a work on the wheels. And the vessel that he made of clay was marred in the hand of the potter: so he made it again another vessel, as seemed good to the potter to make it. Then the word of the Lord came to me, saying, 'O house of Israel, cannot I do with you as this potter? saith the Lord. Behold, as the clay is in the potter's hand, so are ye in mine hand, O house of Israel. At what instant I shall speak concerning a nation, and concerning a kingdom, to pluck up, and to pull down, and to destroy it; If that nation, against whom I have pronounced, turn from their evil, I will repent of the evil that I thought to do unto them. And at what instant I shall speak concerning a nation, and concerning a kingdom, to build and to plant it; If it do evil in my sight, that it obey not my voice, then I will repent of the good, wherewith I said I would benefit them.'"*

Now at first glance, this seems to support my hypothesis. But proponents of Calvinism or Arminianism will point to Paul's reference to this passage in Romans 9. Paul says that God "hath he mercy on whom he will have mercy, and whom he will he hardeneth." Two verses later: "Hath not the potter power over the clay, of the same lump to make one vessel unto honor, and another unto dishonor? What if God, willing to shew his wrath, and to make his power known, endured with much longsuffering the vessels of wrath fitted to destruction. And that he might make known the riches of his glory on the vessels of mercy, which he had afore prepared unto glory." They say that this shows that God not only foreknows but determines who will be saved.

The first point to be made here is that this is in stark opposition to other scriptures that speak of God's salvation applying to everyone, like 1st Timothy 2:4 or 2nd Peter 3:9 or John 3:16. But that's okay, because when we look at the rest of Romans 9, it becomes much less obvious that Paul is referring to predestination. He's talking about how Israel is striving for righteousness by following the law, and failing, because it's impossible to attain righteousness through works. But the Gentiles attained righteousness through faith. I think it's even less likely that Paul is talking about predestination when we look back at the original passage in Jeremiah.

God is showing Jeremiah that, like a potter who remakes his vessel once it gets messed up, God revises his plans when the situation changes. He states quite clearly that he will change his mind about the destruction of Israel *if* they change their ways.

The Bottom Line

My hypothesis isn't a perfect fit with scripture. But it's a good fit. In fact, I think it's a much better fit than classical Calvinism or Arminianism or Molinism. And I maintain that you can hold to biblical inspiration without subscribing to biblical inerrancy.

For example, I have a strong suspicion that God's command to the Israelites to kill women and children and take wives by force in the Promised Land weren't actual commands from God. They were the result of Israelite nationalism. To some, this is too much of a sacrifice. But I wonder why. We can't know that any historical text is one hundred percent accurate, but that doesn't mean we should abandon historical scholarship. The Bible in general and the gospels in particular are some of the most reliable historical texts that exist. I believe them. I believe that Jesus lived, was crucified, and rose again, conquering death and sin.

I also believe that God doesn't know the future. Now that you know my hypothesis, and you know how it fits with God's word, it's time to get to the point. It's time to talk about the implications. It's time to see God, and find love.

CHAPTER 14

GOODNESS IN TIME

Remember back in Chapter 7 when Anselm was trying to reconcile divine foreknowledge and free will? He put forth the argument that we can't define freedom as the ability to sin or not to sin. If that were so, God would not be free. I have two responses to this. First, if we take classical divine omniscience seriously, God is bound in every action by his own knowledge. He can only do what he already knows that he will do (or if he is outside of time entirely, he can do nothing at all in relation to time.) But back when I was studying Anselm, I hadn't looked into theories on time yet, so I didn't have that response ready to go. But I thought of a different one immediately after I read that.

Anselm's reasoning is flawed. Freedom is absolutely the ability to sin or not to sin. God cannot choose to sin because God's essence is goodness. To say that he is not free because he cannot sin is like saying that I am not free because I cannot choose to be an elephant.

God exists. God is good. God is love. God made the universe. God made time. Time is real. The present is all there is. The past is gone forever, and the future has yet to be. God, being omniscient, knows everything. God does not know the future. I've presented my apologetic. I've drawn support from science, philosophy, and scripture itself. Now, let's talk about what it means. Let's face the problem of evil. Let's look it in the eye. Let's solve it.

Facing the Darkness

Let's go back to a time before light, just after the big bang. God has created space and time, and has experienced change, now being related to his creation. The four fundamental forces and universal laws and constants are set in place. Using his guiding hand, God sculpts and molds his universe as a master engineer and artist. Over thirteen billion years later, on (at least) one planet in the vast expanse of space, conditions are right to bring forth a physical organism with a soul, capable of rational thought, and endowed with free will. God calls this organism "man" and names the first one Adam. God, whose essence is love, sets a choice before Adam. A choice between love and hate, good and evil, life and death. (Whether Adam was one man or how many came before him I don't know. It doesn't matter. Humans were in Paradise and then they fell.)

Fast forward to 1940. God's chosen people are being starved, worked to exhaustion, raped, used for experimentation, gassed, and burned alive in death camps in Germany. If Calvinism is true, these events were destined to be from the dawn of time. It was never possible that things would be otherwise. This was part of God's plan. And God works all things together for good. But Calvinism is not true. Calvinism is a lie, and a vicious one. So is Arminianism and Molinism.

I have good news, dear reader. We are not destined for anything. God does not and cannot cause evil. God didn't work good through the Holocaust or the Crusades or 9/11 or any tragedy, evil, or injustice. God didn't give you a disease to bring you closer to him or cause you to rely on him. God doesn't cause pain and suffering. None of this was part of his plan. God doesn't work good through any of these things. God works good *in spite of* them. God doesn't create people knowing their eternal destiny. No one who was ever born was bound for hell. We may echo the apostle Peter that it is God's will that none should perish but all should come to repentance. I say this with no reservations. God is good. God is love.

You've heard it said that there is a purpose for everything. *Far from it!* God did not cause your suffering. Evil caused it. Sin caused it. Sin is a disease. It permeates everything. It is the cause of all moral and natural evil. For the sake of love, God risked. God set forth the choice: the greatest choice. He desired more than anything that we should choose life. And when we did the unthinkable, when we broke the very heart of God, his essence compelled him not to turn his back on us. Rather, he provided a way out. He died. Then he conquered death, so that we could once again, in the midst of our needless and often meaningless pain and suffering, choose life.

Here's more good news. You can and should fight the evil in this world when and where you are able. You should not accept it as part of God's plan. Jesus didn't. He confronted it. He cared for the sick, healed the diseased, fed the hungry, and rebuked evildoers. Then he offered them salvation.

Think about this for a second. Prayer really matters. If you grew up in church like I did, you might have heard a common saying: "Prayer isn't for God, it's for you." Not so! Prayer is most definitely for God. We pray because our prayers have a real and tangible effect on God's decisions. The future is not set. God genuinely listens and cares about what we have to say. He is interested. He wants our input. Granted, we are still God's children, and our Father knows best. God is dealing with innumerable factors far beyond our scope of knowledge. But our prayers and supplications are brought before God because they effect change. God listens and responds.

God is not Aristotle's unmoved mover. God is our ever present help in times of trouble. God is our Savior, our Father, and our friend. The world is dark. It is full of senseless pain and suffering. Full of evil. But God causes all things to work together for good for those that love him.

The Chess Master

Some of you may still be concerned that I have robbed God of his omnipotence. In a sense, you are correct. God could have refrained from creating free creatures. He could have refrained from creating time altogether. But he didn't. We are here. And as a result, God gave up a portion of his control. There is no price that is worth our freedom to God. And in a way, this makes him all the more deserving of our praise and adoration. Perhaps an analogy will help.

Consider the tale of the three chess masters. All three are sitting in a room, facing their respective opponent. The first one is sure he will win. He knows this because he is playing a computer. A computer that he programmed. He knows every move the computer will play before it moves a single piece, because he wrote the code that the computer is using. He wins with ease.

The second chess master is also sure he will win. He's playing a computer too. He didn't write the code for this computer, but he was able to get a copy of it before the game. So sitting in his lap is a piece of paper. Written on it is the script of exactly what the computer will do, and the chess master already knows exactly how he will respond to every move. He wins with ease.

The third chess master is also sure he will win. But the third chess master is playing a person. A real human being. There is no code. There is no script. There is only one player versus another. But this chess master is the best there is. He knows every move that could possibly be made. He knows every strategy. He knows this game inside and out. He doesn't know what his opponent will do, but he knows, whatever it is, he's ready for it. He wins with ease.

Now I ask you, dear reader, which chess master deserves our adoration? To God be the glory, who was and is and is to come. He is good.

ABOUT THE AUTHOR

Ryan Domenick was born and raised in a small town in Western Maryland. Facing a serious of dark events gave rise to his interest in the problem of evil. After researching for the better part of a decade, he crafted a new worldview. He works as an airline pilot in Chicago.